THE AUTHENTIC
Amish
COOKBOOK

Norman and Marlena Miller, Compilers

HARVEST HOUSE PUBLISHERS
EUGENE, OREGON

Cover by Dugan Design Group, Bloomington, Minnesota

Cover photos © sumnersgraphicsinc, Dani Vincek / Fotolia; scorpp / iStockphoto

All Scripture quotations are from the King James Version of the Bible.

Harvest House Publishers has made every effort to trace the ownership of all poems and quotes. In the event of a question arising from the use of a poem or quote, we regret any error made and will be pleased to make the necessary correction in future editions of this book.

THE AUTHENTIC AMISH COOKBOOK
Copyright © 2001 Ridgeway Publishing
Published by Harvest House Publishers
Eugene, Oregon 97402
www.harvesthousepublishers.com

Library of Congress Cataloging-in-Publication Data
   The authentic Amish cookbook / Norman and Marlena Miller, compilers.
      pages cm
   Includes index.
   ISBN 978-0-7369-6365-7 (pbk.)
   ISBN 978-0-7369-6366-4 (eBook)
   1. Amish cooking. 2. Cooking—United States. I. Miller, Norman (Religious writer) II. Miller, Marlena.
   TX721A98 2015
   641.5'66—dc23
                                                              2014023524

Printed in China

19 20 21 22 23 / RDS-JH / 10 9 8 7 6 5 4

Acknowledgments

We wish to express our sincere appreciation
to all who have participated in this project by contributing recipes
and giving support and encouragement.

May you greatly enjoy this book, and
most important of all, we trust your heart will be
drawn closer to God by meditating on the many soul-searching
and thought-provoking inspirations and hymns.

May God richly bless you!
Norman and Marlena Miller

Contents

Sources:

Perma-flo and ThermFlo may be purchased at:
    E & S Sales
    1265 N. St. Rd. 5
    Shipshewana, IN 46565

Appetizers and Beverages

What a Friend We Have in Jesus

There is a friend that sticketh closer than a brother. —Proverbs 18:24

Joseph M. Scriven, 1819-1886   Charles C. Converse, 1832-1918

1. What a friend we have in Je - sus,   All our sins and griefs to bear;
2. Have we tri - als and temp - ta - tions?   Is there troub-le an - y - where?
3. Are we weak and heav - y la - den,   Cum-bered with a load of care?

What a priv - i - lege to car - ry   Ev - 'ry-thing to God in prayer!
We should nev - er be dis - cour - aged: Take it to the Lord in prayer!
Pre - cious Sav-iour, still our ref - uge;   Take it to the Lord in prayer!

O what peace we oft - en for - feit,   O what need-less pain we bear,
Can we find a friend so faith - ful,   Who will all our sor-rows share?
Do thy friends de-spise, for-sake thee?   Take it to the Lord in prayer!

All be-cause we do not car - ry   Ev - 'ry-thing to God in prayer.
Je - sus knows our ev - 'ry weak-ness;   Take it to the Lord in prayer!
In His arms He'll take and shield thee,   Thou wilt find a sol - ace there.

Fruit Slush

1½ to 2 c. sugar
3 c. hot water

6 oz. frozen orange juice concentrate
3 ripe bananas
20-oz. can crushed pineapple

Mix sugar and water; let cool. Add orange juice and 1 can water. Crush 3 ripe bananas and add this and the pineapple plus its juice. Freeze until hard. Delicious!

Mrs. James (Rosanna) Miller

Fruit Dip

8 oz. cream cheese
1 c. marshmallow creme

12 oz. Cool Whip

Mix until smooth. Serve with fresh fruit.

Mrs. Steve (Edith) Engbretson

Crockpot Chip Dip

1 to 1½ lb. hamburger (may add
  some refried beans)
1 onion
salt and pepper to taste
8 oz. taco sauce or salsa
1 can mushroom soup

1 can tomato soup
1 tsp. chili powder
1 tsp. Worcestershire sauce
½ tsp. garlic powder
1 to 1½ lb. Velveeta cheese

Brown hamburger; add rest of ingredients and heat until cheese is melted. Dip tortilla chips. Very delicious! Serves 20.

Miriam Hershberger

I hope my children look back on today,
And see a mom who had time to play.
There will be years for cleaning and cooking,
For children grow up while we're not looking.

. . .

Little things can often be the biggest things
in someone's day.

Taco Dip

2 8-oz. pkg. cream cheese
1 pint container onion chip dip
1 lb. browned hamburger mixed
  with ½ pkg. taco seasoning mix

green peppers, chopped
mushrooms, drained
mild cheddar cheese

Mix cream cheese and onion dip and spread in 9 x 13-inch pan. Spread hamburger/ taco seasoning mix on top of cream cheese mixture and top with green peppers, mushrooms, and cheese. Warm to desired warmth at 250°. Serve with taco chips. Serves 12.

Mrs. Jr. (Esther) Wengerd

Chip and Vegetable Dip

1⅓ c. mayonnaise
2 rounded T. sour cream
onion powder, garlic powder, and onion salt to taste

1 8-oz. pkg. cream cheese

Blend together.

Mrs. Dewayne (Edna Sue) Miller

Ham Roll-Ups

12 oz. cream cheese, softened
1 c. shredded carrots
4 tsp. dill weed

2 tsp. celery flakes
1 lb. fully cooked, thinly sliced ham

In a bowl, combine the cream cheese, carrots, dill weed, and celery flakes. Spread about 2 T. on each slice of ham. Roll up tightly and wrap in plastic wrap. Refrigerate overnight. Slice into 1-inch pieces. Yields 6-7 dozen.

Mrs. Omer (Martha) Miller

Faith never knows where it is being led,
it knows and loves the One who is leading.
It is a life of faith, not of intelligence and reason,
but a life of knowing who is making me "go."
Oswald Chambers

Sweet Potato Bonbons

3 lb. sweet potatoes, peeled and cooked	½ tsp. grated orange rind
¼ c. margarine	6 marshmallows, halved
½ c. brown sugar, firmly packed	⅓ c. melted margarine
1 tsp. salt	4 c. cornflakes, crushed
	12 pecan halves

Mash sweet potatoes until light and fluffy. Beat in ¼ c. margarine, brown sugar, salt, and orange rind. Let cool. Divide into 12 portions. Press potatoes around each marshmallow half, being careful to keep marshmallow in center. Shape into ovals. Coat with ⅓ c. melted margarine. Roll in crushed cornflakes. Top with pecan halves and place on lightly greased baking sheet. Bake in very hot oven at 450° for 7-8 minutes. Serves 6-8.

Mrs. Ben (Keturah) Troyer

Orange Shakes

1 6-oz. can frozen orange juice concentrate

½ c. sugar	1 c. water
1 tsp. vanilla	8 to 10 ice cubes
1 c. milk	

Blend in blender until thick and slushy. Serves 4.

Kathryn Mary Kauffman

Ice Slush

2 3-oz. pkg. Jell-O (cherry, orange, lemon, or lime)	
2 c. sugar	2 c. cold water
1 qt. boiling water	46 oz. pineapple juice

Dissolve Jell-O and sugar in boiling water. Then add cold water and pineapple juice. Freeze. Fill glass ¾ full of slush, then fill up with 7UP. Makes a 5-qt. ice-cream pail almost full. Refreshing in 90° weather.

Mrs. Orlie (Mary) Troyer

Love begins when another person's needs become more important than your own.

Slush Drink

6 oz. Jell-O, any kind
2 c. sugar
6 c. boiling water

46 oz. pineapple juice
6 c. cold water

Dissolve Jell-O and sugar in boiling water; add rest of ingredients and freeze, stirring occasionally. Should be slushy. Serve with Sprite or 7UP. Very refreshing!

Deborah Slabaugh

Spiced Cranberry Tea

1 c. sugar
24 whole cloves
6 oz. cinnamon Red Hots
12 oz. frozen pineapple juice concentrate
12 oz. frozen lemonade concentrate
12 oz. frozen orange juice concentrate

4 c. water
1½ qt. cranberry juice cocktail
stick cinnamon

Boil sugar, water, cloves, and Red Hots until Red Hots dissolve. Add frozen juices and cranberry juice. Now add water equal to the juices, and a 6-inch piece of stick cinnamon. Heat to simmering gently and simmer 5 minutes Remove cloves and cinnamon after it's spicy enough for you. Serve hot on a cold winter day. This is a delicious drink that tastes as good as it smells.

Mrs. Stephen (Amelia) Miller

Punch

5 pkg. cherry Kool-Aid
5 pkg. strawberry Kool-Aid
5 12-oz. cans frozen orange juice
5 12-oz. cans frozen lemon juice

30 oz. 7UP
10 c. sugar
4 gal. water

Add ice and enjoy.

Mrs. Dewayne (Edna Sue) Miller

Abundant living: Think deeply, speak gently, laugh often, work hard, give freely, pay promptly, pray earnestly, and be kind.

Root Beer

2 c. sugar
4½ tsp. root beer extract

½ tsp. yeast, dissolved in warm water

Place ingredients in gallon jar and fill with lukewarm water. Let stand in a warm place for 12 hours, then refrigerate. Don't turn lid on too tightly.

Ruth Maria Herschberger

Hot Chocolate

¼ c. brown sugar
1 T. cocoa
⅓ c. water

4 c. milk
1 tsp. maple syrup or maple flavoring
8 to 10 large marshmallows

Cook sugar and cocoa with water; let bubble for a few minutes, then add milk, marshmallows, and syrup. Cook until marshmallows are melted.

Keturah Engbretson

Maple Hot Chocolate

¼ c. sugar
1 T. baking cocoa
⅛ tsp. salt
¼ c. hot water
1 T. butter or margarine

4 c. milk
1 tsp. maple flavoring
1 tsp. vanilla extract
12 large marshmallows

In a large saucepan, combine sugar, cocoa, and salt. Stir in hot water and butter; bring to a boil. Add the milk, maple flavoring, vanilla, and 8 marshmallows. Heat through, stirring occasionally, until marshmallows are melted. Ladle into mugs and top each with a marshmallow. Serves 4.

Mrs. Norman (Marlena) Miller

Nature forms us

Sin deforms us

School informs us

Christ transforms us

Chocolate Syrup

4 c. brown sugar (scant)
2 c. cocoa
½ c. corn syrup

4 c. white sugar
2 c. water
¼ c. vanilla

Mix all ingredients except vanilla in a 6-quart kettle until all is blended. Add 2 more cups of water and stir again. Bring to a boil and boil for 5 minutes (it is very likely to boil over). Add vanilla. If not canned, put cover on until cool or a crust will form over the top. This will keep from September to April (school months) if put boiling hot into jars and sealed. Yields approximately 3 quarts.

Mrs. Leroy (Viola) Mast

Salads and Salad Dressings

Precious Memories

J.B.F. Wright, b. 1877   J.B.F. Wright, b. 1877

1. Pre-cious mem'ries, un - seen an - gels, Sent from somewhere to my soul;
2. Pre-cious fa - ther, lov - ing moth-er, Fly   a - cross the lone - ly years,
3. In   the still-ness of   the midnight, Ech - oes from the past I hear;
4. As   I trav - el on life's pathway, Know not what the years may hold,

How they lin - ger, ev - er near me, And the sa - cred past un - fold.
And   old home scenes of   my child-hood, In   fond mem - o - ry ap-pears.
Old - time sing - ing, glad - ness bring-ing, From that love - ly land somewhere.
As   I   pon - der, hope grows fond - er, Pre - cious mem'ries flood my soul.

REFRAIN

Pre-cious mem'ries, How they lin - ger, How they ev - er flood my soul,

In   the still-ness of   the mid-night, Pre - cious, sa - cred scenes un-fold.

Apple Salad Dressing

1 c. sugar
1 egg
2 T. flour
1 T. vinegar

1 T. margarine
1 c. water
pinch of salt

Mix sugar, flour, and egg in small saucepan. Stir in water and add margarine. Boil until slightly thickened, then add vinegar and salt. Cool before pouring over apples. Raisins, marshmallows, nuts, cheese, grapes, and/or pineapple may be added if you have them on hand. Store any remaining dressing in covered jar in refrigerator.

Mrs. Marcus (Mary) Gingerich
Marjorie Mast

Apple Salad Dressing

1 c. water
½ c. sugar
2 T. flour
1 egg

1 tsp. vanilla
1 tsp. vinegar
½ tsp. lemon juice (optional)

Bring water to boiling point. Beat egg, sugar, and flour together to form a smooth paste. Stir into boiling water and cook 1 to 2 minutes. Remove from heat and add vinegar, vanilla, and lemon juice if desired. Chill. Pour over apples, pineapple, nuts, or fresh fruit of your choice like bananas, grapes, or oranges.

Mrs. Noah (Fannie) Yoder

Thank God for dirty dishes,
They have a tale to tell;
While other folks go hungry,
We're eating very well.
With home and happiness,
We shouldn't want to fuss;
For by this stack of evidence,
God's very good to us.

Apple Salad Dressing

2 c. sugar
2 eggs
2 heaping T. flour

2 scant tsp. vinegar
2 c. water
½ tsp. salt

Beat eggs and stir in sugar, flour, and salt. Then add water and vinegar. Cook until thickened. Then add 1 T. butter and 2 T. vanilla when it's cooked. Pour over apples, celery, nuts, cheese, pineapple, and raisins or grapes. Oranges or canned fruit may also be used.

Mrs. Alva (Elnora) Hochstetler

Fruit Salad

1 qt. fruit juice or water
2 eggs
2 c. sugar
5 T. flour

1 tsp. vanilla
2 T. vinegar
2 T. butter

Heat 3 c. of the fruit juice, vinegar, and butter. Stir together sugar and flour and beat in eggs. Stir in reserved cup of the juice; beat. Add to hot fruit juice along with vanilla and stir until thick. Cool. Pour over chopped apples, sliced grapes, pineapple, mini marshmallows, raisins, etc. Mix. I use red and yellow apples and leave them unpeeled for color and fiber.

Beth Ann Yoder

God's Good Gifts

God's mercies are new every morning,
God's grace is born fresh with the day.
God's good gifts are all freely given,
To use every step of the way.

God's peace is deep, quiet, and constant,
Eternal as heaven above.
May you always know as through life you go,
The good gifts that God sends in love.

Overnight Fruit Salad

3 eggs, beaten
¼ c. sugar
¼ c. vinegar
2 T. butter or margarine
2 c. green grapes
2 c. miniature marshmallows
2 medium, firm bananas, sliced

1 20-oz. can pineapple chunks,
    drained
1 15-oz. can mandarin oranges,
    drained
2 c. whipping cream, whipped
½ c. chopped pecans

In a double boiler over medium heat, cook and stir eggs, sugar, and vinegar until mixture is thickened and reaches 160°. Remove from heat; stir in butter. Cool. In a large serving bowl, combine grapes, marshmallows, pineapple, oranges, and bananas; add cooled dressing and stir to coat. Refrigerate for 4 hours or overnight. Just before serving, fold in whipped cream and pecans. Serves 12-16.

Mrs. Jerome (Rose) Graber

Sunshine Salad

1st layer:
2 3-oz. boxes lemon Jell-O dissolved in 4 c. water. When starting to jell, add 1 can crushed pineapple, drained. Save juice.
2nd layer:
1 8-oz. pkg. cream cheese   1 12-oz. container Cool Whip
Mix until smooth; put on first layer after it sets.
3rd layer:
To juice of pineapple add 1 c. sugar and water to make 1½ c. Stir in 3 T. flour, 3 egg yolks, and pinch of salt. Cook until smooth; cool. Put on top.

Put in 9 x 13-inch pan. Refrigerate and serve. Serves 12.

Ruth Wengerd

God grant me the serenity to accept the things I cannot change, the courage to change the things I can, and the wisdom to know the difference.

Reinhold Niebuhr

. . .

Daily prayers lessen daily cares.

Creamy Golden Salad

2 c. boiling water
1 6-oz. pkg. lemon Jell-O
1 c. miniature marshmallows
8 oz. cream cheese

2 c. Cool Whip
1 20-oz. can crushed pineapple,
 drained

Dissolve Jell-O in water. Add marshmallows and cream cheese. Beat well with beater. Add Cool Whip and pineapple. Pour into 2-qt. Jell-O mold. Refrigerate until set.

Mrs. Omer (Martha) Miller

Buttermilk Salad

2 small pkg. cherry Jell-O
1 can pineapple
2 c. buttermilk

4 c. whipped cream
½ c. nuts (optional)

Heat pineapple juice and dissolve Jell-O in it. Add rest of ingredients; cool until set.

Mrs. John (Fannie) Miller

Hidden Pear Salad

1 16-oz. can pears, liquid
 drained and reserved
1 3-oz. pkg. lime flavored Jell-O

1 3-oz. pkg. cream cheese, softened
¼ tsp. lemon juice
1 8-oz. container Cool Whip

In a saucepan, bring pear liquid to a boil. Stir in gelatin until dissolved. Remove from heat and cool at room temperature until syrupy. Meanwhile puree pears in a blender. In a mixing bowl, beat cream cheese and lemon juice until fluffy and smooth. Add pureed pears and mix well. Fold Cool Whip into pear mixture. Fold in cooled gelatin. Pour into an oiled 4½-c. mold; chill overnight. Just before serving, unmold salad onto a plate. Serves 6-8.

Mrs. Jerome (Rose) Graber

A duty dodged is like a debt unpaid; it is only deferred, and we must come back and settle the account at last.

Joseph F. Newton

Pear Salad

1 qt. canned pears, drained
2 c. boiling water
6 oz. lime Jell-O

8 oz. cream cheese
1 c. miniature marshmallows
8 oz. frozen whipped topping

Pour boiling water over Jell-O. Stir until dissolved. Blend pears in Salsa Master or food processor until smooth. Add marshmallows to Jell-O. Add cream cheese, pears, and whipped topping. Beat well with beater. Pour into serving bowl.

Mrs. Omer (Martha) Miller

Triple Orange Salad

1 box orange Jell-O
1 box instant vanilla pudding
1 box tapioca pudding

2½ c. water
1 can mandarin oranges, drained
2 c. Cool Whip

Bring Jell-O, puddings, and water to a full boil, then take from heat and cool. Add mandarin oranges and Cool Whip.

Mrs. John (Carolyn) Otto

Jazzy Gelatin

1 6-oz. pkg. orange gelatin
2 c. boiling water
1 c. ice cubes
1 15-oz. can mandarin oranges,
   drained

1 8-oz. can unsweetened crushed
   pineapple, undrained
1 6-oz. can frozen orange juice
   concentrate, thawed
green grapes and fresh mint
   for center, optional

In a bowl, dissolve gelatin in boiling water. Add ice cubes, oranges, pineapple, and orange juice concentrate. Pour into a 6-cup ring mold coated with nonstick cooking spray. Refrigerate overnight or until firm. Just before serving, unmold onto a serving plate. If desired fill center with grapes and garnish with mint. Serves 12.

Esther Delagrange

Thou hast given us so much, dear Lord, but give us one thing more—a grateful heart.

Apricot Salad

2 3-oz. boxes apricot Jell-O
2 c. boiling water
2 c. cold water
1 c. miniature marshmallows
1 20-oz. can crushed pineapple,
    drained
1 egg

1 8-oz. container whipped topping
2 bananas, diced
½ c. pineapple juice
½ c. sugar
2 T. flour
2 T. butter
1 8-oz. pkg. cream cheese

Dissolve Jell-O in boiling water, then add cold water and marshmallows. Add drained pineapple and bananas. Let jell. Topping: Take juice from pineapple, sugar, flour, butter, and egg and cook until thickened. Cool, then fold cream cheese and whipped topping into thickened sauce. Spread over Jell-O. Let set overnight. Variation: Orange Jell-O may also be used.

Mrs. Norman (Marlena) Miller

Cinnamon Applesauce Ring

¼ c. Red Hot candies
1 c. water
2 c. thick applesauce

1 pkg. cherry Jell-O
1 container cottage cheese

Combine candies and water. Heat to boiling or until candies are dissolved. Remove from heat. Add Jell-O. Stir and cool slightly. Add applesauce. Pour into 1-quart mold. Chill until firm. Serve with cottage cheese. Serves 10-12.

Mrs. Ben (Keturah) Troyer

Lime Jell-O Salad

64 large marshmallows
4 c. milk
2 c. lime Jell-O
2 lb. cottage cheese

1 c. Miracle Whip dressing
2 c. whipped cream
1 20-oz. can pineapple

Combine marshmallows and milk in double boiler and heat until marshmallows melt; pour over Jell-O and stir until dissolved. When partially set, add remaining ingredients. This makes 4 qt. salad. Serves 32.

Mrs. Michael (Lydia Ann) Stoll

7UP Jell-O Pudding

2 3-oz. boxes lemon Jell-O
2 c. 7UP pop
2 c. boiling water
2 large bananas
1 can crushed pineapple, drained
marshmallows

1 c. pineapple juice
1 c. sugar
2 T. flour
1 egg
2 T. butter
1 c. whipped cream

Put together boiling water, Jell-O, and pop. Add fruit and marshmallows after Jell-O starts to set. Boil together pineapple juice, sugar, flour, egg, and butter. Cool. Add whipped cream. Put on top of set Jell-O. Serves 6.

Mrs. Ernest (Mary Ellen) Miller

Taco Salad

1 medium head of lettuce
1 small can kidney beans
1 medium onion
8 oz. cheddar cheese
4 medium tomatoes, diced
1 pkg. taco chips
1 lb. hamburger, browned

1 pkg. taco seasoning

Dressing:
8 oz. Thousand Island dressing
⅓ c. sugar
1 T. taco seasoning
1 T. taco sauce

Brown hamburger (add taco seasoning, reserving 1 tablespoon for dressing). Cool. Cut up lettuce as for tossed salad. Layer ingredients in salad bowl. Rinse and drain kidney beans before adding. Add diced tomatoes, chips, and dressing just before serving.

Ruth Maria Herschberger

I still find each day too short for all the thoughts I want to think; all the walks I want to take; all the books I want to read; and all the friends I want to see.

John Burroughs

Taco Salad

1 lb. hamburger	shredded cheese
1 15-oz. can kidney beans	2 large tomatoes
1 onion	½ pkg. taco seasoning
1 head lettuce	½ pkg. taco chips

Brown hamburger with onion, add taco seasoning. Blend everything together except dressing.

Thousand Island Dressing:

1 c. Miracle Whip dressing	¾ tsp. salt
½ c. sugar	½ tsp. paprika
¼ c. vinegar	½ tsp. black pepper
¼ c. catsup	¼ tsp. garlic powder
2 T. oil	2 T. taco seasoning

Blend well.

Regina Miller

Taco Salad

1 lb. hamburger	1 pkg. taco seasoning
1 medium onion, chopped	1 pint kidney beans
4 oz. Velveeta cheese	¼ tsp. salt
8 oz. Thousand Island dressing	

Thousand Island Dressing:

2 c. Miracle Whip dressing	pepper
½ c. ketchup	paprika
¼ tsp. salt	garlic salt

Fry hamburger and onion; drain. Add remaining ingredients. Simmer and serve over cut up lettuce and tomatoes. Top with broken taco chips.

Mrs. David (Rhoda) Miller

To lose your wealth is much.
To lose your health is more.
To lose your soul is such a loss,
That nothing can restore.

Italian Macaroni Salad

8 oz. spiral macaroni noodles
green onions, chopped
green peppers, sliced
black olives, sliced
tomatoes, diced, optional
carrots, shredded, optional
shredded mozzarella or
   cheddar cheese, optional

½ c. olive oil
¼ c. vinegar
1 tsp. sugar
1 tsp. each minced onion and garlic
½ tsp. each oregano, basil,
   and parsley
½ c. Parmesan cheese

Cook noodles until just done, drain, rinse, and cool immediately. Mix noodles and vegetables (cheese, if desired) in medium-size bowl. In separate small bowl, mix rest of ingredients. Pour over noodle mixture and toss. Serves 4.

Mrs. Reuben (Elizabeth) Luthy

Surprise Cabbage Salad

6 oz. lemon and lime Jell-O
2 c. boiling water
1 c. small marshmallows
¾ c. Miracle Whip dressing
1 c. pineapple juice

1 c. crushed pineapple
1½ c. shredded cabbage
1 c. whipped cream
1 c. nuts, chopped

Dissolve Jell-O in water; add marshmallows while hot and stir until dissolved. Add salad dressing, pineapple and juice, and cabbage. Let stand in refrigerator until it starts to set. Then add whipped cream and nuts.

Mrs. James (Rosanna) Miller

Cottage Cheese Salad

1 c. milk
1 large pkg. marshmallows
½ c. sugar
1 envelope unflavored gelatin
1 8-oz. pkg. cream cheese

1 c. cream, whipped and sweetened
1 c. crushed pineapple
2 lb. cottage cheese
1 tsp. vanilla

Soak gelatin in small amount of water. Heat milk, marshmallows, and sugar together. Add gelatin and stir until dissolved. Cool until slightly jelled, then add remaining ingredients. Mix and pour into a pan and let set.

Lena Yoder

Recipe for Friendship

2 heaping cups patience
1 heart full of love
2 handfuls of generosity

dash of laughter
1 full cup of understanding
2 cups of loyalty

Take all the above ingredients and mix well. Sprinkle generously with kindness. Spread this irresistible delicacy over a lifetime and serve everybody you meet.

Ribbon Salad

2 3-oz. pkg. lime Jell-O
5 c. boiling water
1 8-oz. pkg. cream cheese
1 c. heavy whipping cream, whipped
1 c. Miracle Whip dressing
2 3-oz. pkg. cherry Jell-O

½ c. miniature marshmallows,
    cut up
4 c. cold water
1 1 lb.-4 oz. can crushed pineapple
1 3-oz. pkg. lemon Jell-O

Dissolve lime Jell-O in 2 c. of the boiling water in a bowl. Stir in 2 c. of the cold water. Pour into 9 x 13 x 2-inch pan. Chill until partially set. Drain pineapple, reserving 1 c. juice. Set aside. Dissolve lemon Jell-O in 1 c. boiling water in a double boiler. Topping: Add marshmallows, place over simmering water. Stir until marshmallows are melted; remove from heat. Add 1 c. reserved juice and cream cheese. Beat with egg beater until well blended. Stir in pineapple, cool. Fold in whipped cream and dressing. Chill until thickened. Pour over lime Jell-O layer. Chill until almost set. Dissolve cherry Jell-O in remaining 2 c. boiling water in a bowl. Stir in remaining 2 c. cold water. Chill until thick and syrupy. Pour over pineapple layer. Chill completely before serving.

Martha Graber

Quick Cottage Cheese

Heat 1 gal. milk to 180°. Add approximately ⅓ c. vinegar while stirring (enough to completely separate). Stir until completely separated. Drain. Rinse with cold water. Chop into small pieces if curds are large. Add rich milk (about half cream) and salt to taste.

Mrs. Jerry (Ruth) Gingerich

The Authentic Amish Cookbook

Cottage Cheese

1 gallon skim milk	salt to taste
4 to 5 T. vinegar	sweet cream

Heat milk in kettle slowly to 190°. Add vinegar, just enough to separate curds from whey. Drain in cheesecloth or colander with fine holes. When well-drained, crumble curds and add salt to suit your taste. Chill and add sweet cream before serving. Garnish with black pepper or parsley flakes, etc. Delicious served with fruit or topped with maple syrup!

Mrs. Marcus (Mary) Gingerich

24-Hour Potato Salad

12 c. potatoes, cooked and cut up	6 T. mustard
12 eggs, chopped	2 tsp. salt
½ medium onion, chopped	1½ c. white sugar
2 c. celery, chopped	¼ c. vinegar
3 c. Miracle Whip dressing	½ c. milk

Mix together first 4 ingredients, then make a dressing with all other ingredients and put together. This can be made a few days ahead.

Esther Miller

Potato Salad

14 c. potatoes, shredded	3 T. mustard
10 eggs, cooked and chopped	¼ c. vinegar
½ medium onion	½ c. milk
2 c. chopped celery	1½ c. sugar
3 c. Miracle Whip dressing	4 tsp. salt

Mix together first 4 ingredients, then make a dressing with all other ingredients and mix together. One batch makes about 5 quarts.

Mrs. Glen (Marilyn) Miller

A clear conscience is a soft pillow.
German Proverb

. . .

Cheerfulness, joy, and contentment
are preservers of youthful looks.

Roasted Potato Salad

12 red skin potatoes
1 c. Miracle Whip
4 boiled eggs
1 pkg. fried bacon

½ c. finely chopped onion
(optional)
salt and pepper to taste

Quarter potatoes, lay skin side down onto a well-greased cookie sheet. Roast in oven at 350° until tender and golden. While potatoes are cooking, gather rest of ingredients and cut up boiled eggs and onion. Crumble fried bacon into pieces. When potatoes are finished, immediately fold in Miracle Whip, then rest of ingredients. This dish is best served when hot. Delicious!

Mrs. Gregory (Denise) Rich

Lettuce Dressing

2 c. white sugar
2 c. vegetable oil
¾ c. ketchup
⅓ c. vinegar

2 tsp. Worcestershire sauce
1 c. Miracle Whip dressing
pinch salt
a little onion, cut fine

Beat all together.

Mrs. Edna Slabaugh

Layer Lettuce Salad

1 head lettuce
1 c. diced celery
4 eggs, hard-boiled and sliced
10 oz. pkg. frozen peas
bacon bits or 8 slices bacon, fried

1 medium onion, diced
2 c. Miracle Whip, mixed with
  2 T. sugar
4 oz. grated cheddar cheese
½ c. green pepper, diced (optional)

Put in 9 x 13-inch glass dish. Place lettuce in bottom of dish in bite-sized pieces. Add rest of ingredients in order given. Put Miracle Whip mixture over the top like icing. Sprinkle with grated cheese. Cover with plastic wrap and refrigerate 8 to 12 hours before serving. Sprinkle bacon bits on top before serving.

Mrs. John (Carolyn) Otto
Mrs. Mahlon (Wanita Kay) Bontrager

Minted Pea Salad

½ c. mayonnaise
¼ c. sour cream
¼ c. minced fresh mint
¾ tsp. salt

dash pepper
3 c. frozen peas (thawed) or
   3 c. fresh, blanched peas
1 small onion, finely chopped

In a bowl combine the first five ingredients. Mix well. Add peas and onion; toss to coat. Cover and refrigerate 1 hour. Serves 4-6.

Mrs. Omer (Martha) Miller

Spinach Mushroom Salad

1 lb. spinach, torn up
3 oz. mushrooms
   Dressing:
⅓ c. oil
¼ c. vinegar
¼ tsp. salt

2 slices bacon
1 hard-boiled egg

fresh ground pepper
1 clove garlic, crushed

Shake dressing ingredients in a jar. Arrange spinach on a large plate or pan with mushrooms on top. Pour dressing over salad and garnish with bacon and egg. I usually make it without garlic or bacon and use more eggs and mushrooms. Serves about 6.

Mrs. Elvie (Rebekah) Miller

Doing nothing is the most tiresome job because you can't quit and rest.

. . .

A happy home is not without problems, but one that handles them with love and understanding.

Notes

Breads, Rolls, and Cereals

Gott ist die Liebe

Aug. Rische, 1819-1906

Thuringer Volksweise, 1840

1. Gott ist die Lie - be, Lässt mich er - lö - sen;
2. Ich lag in Ban - den Der schnö - den Sün - den;
3. Je - sus, mein Hei - land, Gab Sich zum Op - fer;
4. O süs - se Lie - be, Du Brunn des Hei - les;
5. Dich will ich prei - sen, Du ew' - ge Lie - be;

Gott ist die Lie - be, Er liebt auch mich.
Ich lag in Ban - den Und konnt nicht los.
Je - sus, mein Hei - land, Büsst mei - ne Schuld.
O süs - se Lie - be, Der See - len Trost.
Dich will ich lo - ben, So lang ich bin.

REFRAIN

Drum sag' ich noch ein - mal: Gott ist die Lie - be,

Gott ist die Lie - be, Er liebt auch mich.

Light Wheat Bread

6 c. lukewarm water
1½ T. salt
⅔ c. white sugar
3 T. yeast

4 c. fine whole wheat flour
½ c. canola oil
11 c. bread flour (white)

Mix together first 6 ingredients with beater; add 4 cups white flour. Stir. Add rest of flour; knead 10 minutes. Let rise 30 minutes. Punch down. Repeat 3 more times. Roll out 6 loaves and put in greased pans. Let rise. Bake at 350° for 35 minutes. Cool on wire racks. Makes 6 loaves.

Mrs. Omer (Martha) Miller

Bread

2 c. warm water
2 T. yeast
1 egg
½ c. sugar

⅓ c. vegetable oil
2 T. salt
7 c. bread flour

Mix together yeast, sugar, and salt; add warm water and mix together; add oil and egg. Begin adding flour, mixing well after each addition. Knead for 10 minutes. Let rise for 30 minutes. Form into loaves. Let rise 45 minutes. Bake at 400° for 25 to 30 minutes. Makes 2 loaves.

Beth Ann Yoder

You can't keep trouble from coming, but you needn't give it a chair to sit on.

. . .

Peace rules the day when Christ rules the mind.

Butterhorns

1½ c. scalded milk	1 T. yeast
1 c. vegetable oil	2 tsp. sugar
½ c. sugar	½ c. warm water
1 tsp. salt	5½ c. flour
3 eggs	

Mix first four ingredients together; let cool. Dissolve yeast in warm water with 2 tsp. sugar; add to milk mixture and beat well. Add 2 c. flour, then beat in 3 eggs. Now add remaining 3½ c. flour. Refrigerate overnight. Divide into 4 parts. Don't knead, just pat or roll into shape of a pie. Use plenty of flour to roll out. Spread well with browned butter. Cut each pie into 16 parts. Roll up as crescents. Let rise about 2 hours. Bake at 375° for 15 minutes. They need not brown much. Ice with powdered sugar icing if you care to serve as sweet rolls.

Marilyn Kay Herschberger

Crescent Dinner Rolls

1 c. milk	¼ c. margarine
¼ c. sugar	½ c. warm water
1 tsp. salt	2 T. yeast
2 eggs, beaten	5¼ c. flour (approximately)

Scald milk; add sugar, salt, and margarine. Measure warm water into large bowl, add yeast. Add milk mixture, eggs, and 2 cups flour. Beat until smooth. Add rest of flour to make soft dough. Let rise until double in bulk. Roll into circles. Spread with soft margarine. Cut into pie-shaped wedges. Roll up wedges, starting at wide end. Let rise; bake at 350° until golden.

Mrs. Earl (Irma) Chupp

Oatmeal Muffins

1 c. cooked oatmeal	½ tsp. salt
1½ c. flour	1 egg
3 T. sugar	¼ c. melted butter
3 tsp. baking powder	½ c. milk

Blend dry ingredients, and then work oatmeal in with pastry blender (or spoon). Beat egg with milk. Gradually add to dry ingredients with melted butter. Makes 12 muffins. Bake at 350° for 25 minutes.

Mrs. John (Fannie) Miller

Blueberry Muffins

2 c. flour
4 tsp. baking powder
½ tsp. salt
4 T. sugar

2 T. melted butter
1 egg, beaten
1 c. milk
1 c. blueberries

Sift flour, reserving 3 tablespoons to dust berries. To remaining flour, add baking powder, salt, and sugar. Sift again. Add beaten egg and melted butter to milk and combine with dry ingredients. Fold in dusted berries. Drop by spoonfuls in greased muffin tins. Bake at 425° for 25 minutes. Yields 10-12 muffins.

Rita Miller

Feather-Light Muffins

⅓ c. shortening
½ c. sugar
1 egg
1½ c. cake flour
1½ tsp. baking powder
½ tsp. salt
¼ tsp. ground nutmeg

½ c. milk

Topping:
½ c. sugar
1 tsp. cinnamon
½ c. melted butter

In a mixing bowl, cream shortening, sugar, and egg. Combine dry ingredients; add to creamed mixture alternately with milk. Fill greased muffin tins ⅔ full. Bake at 325° for 25 minutes. Let cool for 3 to 4 minutes. Meanwhile, combine sugar and cinnamon in a small bowl. Roll warm muffins in melted butter, then in sugar mixture. Serve warm. Serves 8-10.

Ruby Chupp

Easy Cinnamon Rolls

1 box yellow cake mix
2 pkg. dry yeast
1 tsp. salt
2½ c. warm water

5 c. flour
¼ c. butter, melted
1 to 2 T. cinnamon
¼ c. sugar

Stir together salt and water. Combine cake mix and yeast. Add to salt water. Add flour and mix well. Cover bowl with plastic wrap and let rise 1 hour or until it has doubled in bulk. Punch down and then pat into rectangle. Spread butter on dough and then sprinkle on cinnamon and sugar. Roll up jelly-roll style and cut into rolls. Let rise again. Bake at 350° for 20 minutes or until they test done.

Mrs. Wilbur (Joann) Hochstetler

Cinnamon Rolls

1 c. scalded milk	½ tsp. salt
1 c. lukewarm water	½ c. shortening
2 eggs, beaten	2 T. yeast, or 2 pkgs.
½ c. sugar	7 c. flour

Soak yeast in warm water, cool milk to warm. Beat in eggs, sugar, salt, and shortening. Add flour. Stir until real stiff and let rise for 2 hours. Roll out and spread with butter, brown sugar, and cinnamon. Cut slices and place in greased pans. Let rise 1 hour. Bake at 350° for 15-20 minutes.

Mrs. Alva (Elnora) Hochstetler

Cinnamon Rolls

1 c. milk, scalded	2 eggs, beaten
½ c. margarine	1 T. yeast, dissolved in
⅓ c. sugar	¼ c. warm water
½ tsp. salt	4 c. flour

Mix all together; place in a covered bowl in refrigerator overnight. Next morning roll out dough and spread with butter, brown sugar, and cinnamon. Roll up and then cut slices and place in greased pans. Let rise until double. Bake at 350° for 20-25 minutes.

Mrs. Omer (Martha) Miller

Cinnamon Rolls

8 T. yeast	8 tsp. salt
1 qt. milk, scalded	1 lb. margarine
1 c. warm water	8 eggs
2 c. brown sugar	15 c. flour

Mix together all ingredients. Let rise an hour, then roll out and put on more margarine, brown sugar, and cinnamon. Roll up and cut and put on greased cookie sheet. Bake at 350° for 20 minutes. Rotate after 10 minutes.

Mrs. Ernest (Mary Ellen) Miller

What is done can never be undone. But what is broken can be fixed by God's grace.

Cinnamon Rolls

1 T. sugar	6 eggs
1 c. water (warm)	1 c. lard
5 T. yeast	1¼ c. sugar
1 T. salt	1 qt. donut mix
1½ qt. water (warm)	3 qt. + 1 c. flour

Mix first 3 ingredients together and let rise. Cream together sugar, eggs, lard, and salt. Add water, donut mix, and yeast mixture. Then add flour. Let rise one hour. Then roll out, spread with melted butter, brown sugar, and cinnamon. Roll up and cut, and let rise again. Bake at 350°.

Mrs. John (Carolyn) Otto

Frosting for Cinnamon Rolls

½ c. butter	1 tsp. vanilla
1 lb. powdered sugar	⅛ tsp. salt
1 egg	1 T. milk or cream

Cream butter until smooth. Add ⅓ of sugar and cream; mix thoroughly. Add salt, milk, and vanilla. Blend. Add unbeaten egg and beat until smooth. Add remaining sugar. Add more milk if too thick. Delicious on cinnamon rolls.

Mrs. John (Carolyn) Otto

Potato Doughnuts

1¾ c. milk, scalded	1 T. yeast
½ c. shortening	½ c. warm water
½ c. sugar	6½ to 7 c. flour
½ c. mashed potatoes	1 tsp. baking powder
2 beaten eggs	2 tsp. salt
½ tsp. vanilla	

Scald milk, then stir in shortening, sugar, and potatoes. Cool to lukewarm. Sprinkle 1 T. yeast over ½ c. warm water and stir until dissolved. Add to first mixture; stir in eggs and vanilla. Sift dry ingredients, then gradually add to the milk mixture. This is a soft dough. Let rise until double. Roll out to ½-inch thickness. Cut and deep fat fry in oil. Glaze with powdered sugar and water or roll in cinnamon and sugar mixture. Makes 3 dozen.

Mrs. Jerome (Rose) Graber

Kolaches

2 c. scalded milk	1 T. salt
1 c. lukewarm water	¾ c. oil
2 pkg. dry yeast	2 egg yolks
½ c. sugar	7 to 7½ c. flour

Dissolve yeast in lukewarm water; add milk and other ingredients. Measure flour and add with milk. Let rise; turn out and make into balls. Flatten with palm. Put on greased cookie sheets. Make depression in center and fill with thickened cherries, pineapple, or prunes. Let rise 15 minutes. Bake at 400° until done. Frost while warm. This makes about 3 dozen kolaches.

Rita Miller

Long Johns

(Long Johns)	*(Filling)*
1 pkg. yeast	1½ rounded tsp. flour
¼ c. lukewarm water	½ T. sugar
1 pt. milk	½ c. milk
½ c. sugar	½ tsp. vanilla
½ c. lard	½ c. white sugar
1 tsp. salt	½ c. shortening
6 c. flour	1¼ c. or more powdered sugar

To make Long Johns, dissolve yeast in lukewarm water. Heat milk to boiling point. Add sugar, lard, and salt to hot milk and cool to lukewarm. Then add yeast mixture. Add flour. Cover and let rise. Work it down, let rise again, then roll out and cut in pieces. Let rise and fry in deep fat. To make filling, mix flour and sugar. Then mix with milk and cook. When cold, add vanilla. Cream white sugar and shortening. Then add flavor and milk mixture. Add 1¼ c. or more powdered sugar; cream well. When Long Johns are cooled, cut tops and fill with filling.

Mrs. Mahlon (Wanita Kay) Bontrager

Help me to live from day to day
in such a self-forgetting way,
That even when I kneel to pray,
My prayer may be for others.
. . .
Always try to be a little kinder than necessary.

James Matthew Barrie

Soft Pretzels

1 c. warm water	2 T. sugar
1 T. yeast	1 T. butter, melted
1 tsp. salt	3 c. flour

Measure water into bowl; put yeast in. Stir until melted; add sugar, salt, and butter. Add 2 c. flour; beat well. Stir in enough flour to make a stiff dough. Knead until smooth and elastic, about 5 minutes. Place in greased bowl; grease top and cover. Let rise in draft-free warm place for 40 minutes. Divide dough in half, each half in 6 parts. Roll each piece into a 20-inch-long rope; shape into pretzel. Place on greased cookie sheet, cover and let rise 5 minutes. Dip pretzels in baking soda water (2 tsp. baking soda in 1 pt. warm water). Take pretzel out of water, sprinkle with salt, and bake at 375° for 15 minutes. Dip in butter after removing from oven. Delicious with pizza sauce.

Joanna Miller

Soft Pretzels

1½ c. warm water	4½ c. flour
2 T. dry yeast	1 T. sugar
½ tsp. salt	

Dissolve yeast in warm water; add sugar and mix well. Add rest of ingredients. Let rise in warm place for 15 minutes. Roll out and shape into pretzels. Dip into soda solution of 3 c. boiling water and 4 tsp. baking soda. Keep this on low heat as you dip them. Drain. (They can be drained on a towel.) Place on cookie sheet and sprinkle with pretzel salt or garlic salt, etc. Bake at 450° until golden brown, about 12-14 minutes. Dip in melted butter. Serves 15.

Rachel Wengerd

Corn Bread

2 c. cornmeal	1 tsp. salt
2 c. flour	4 eggs
½ c. sugar	2 c. milk
7 tsp. baking powder, rounded	½ c. vegetable oil

Sift together dry ingredients. Add milk, well-beaten eggs, and vegetable oil. Pour into 9 x 13-inch pan. Bake at 375° for 30 minutes. This is good with gravy.

Marilyn Kay Herschberger

Hush Puppies

1½ c. cornmeal	2 eggs, beaten
1½ c. water	1 c. flour
⅓ c. milk	3 tsp. baking powder
1 T. vegetable oil	2 tsp. salt
2 tsp. grated onion (optional)	1 tsp. sugar (optional)

Cook cornmeal and water until stiff and forms a ball, about 6 minutes. Remove from heat. Add milk, oil, and onion. Stir until smooth. Gradually stir in beaten eggs. Blend dry ingredients and mix well with cornmeal mixture. Drop by teaspoon into 1-inch-deep hot fat.

Mrs. Elvie (Rebekah) Miller

Quick and Easy Pizza Crust

1¾ c. flour	3 T. chopped onion
1½ tsp. salt	¾ c. milk
¾ tsp. baking powder	3 T. cooking oil
¾ tsp. chili powder	2 eggs

Mix well. Press into a well-greased 12 x 16-inch cake pan. Bake at 350° until done, then add pizza toppings.

Martha Graber

Pizza Dough

1 c. milk	1 tsp. salt
¼ c. sugar	1 pkg. yeast
4 T. butter	1 egg
4 c. flour	

Heat milk with sugar, butter, and salt until butter is melted, then cool. Soften yeast in ⅛ c. lukewarm water. When milk is cooled, beat the egg and pour into the milk mixture. Add the yeast mixture and pour all at once into the flour. Beat until mixture is smooth. Let rise in warm place. Roll out thinly and top with toppings of your choice. Bake at 400° for 20 minutes.

Mrs. Nathan (Mattie) Miller

The more we grow up,
the less we blow up.

Orange Cinnamon French Toast

4 T. melted butter
2 T. honey
½ tsp. ground cinnamon

3 beaten eggs
½ c. orange juice
6 slices bread

In a bowl, combine butter, honey, and cinnamon. Pour into 9 x 13-inch pan; spread to coat bottom of pan. Mix together eggs and juice. Dip bread into egg mixture and place in pan, turning bread slices once to coat both sides with honey and butter mixture. Bake at 400° for 15-20 minutes or until golden brown. Serve with additional honey or maple syrup.

Mrs. Omer (Martha) Miller

Chocolate Chip Granola Cereal

6 c. quick oatmeal
2 c. brown sugar
2 tsp. salt
1½ c. melted butter

4 c. whole wheat flour
1 c. coconut (optional)
1½ tsp. baking soda
1 c. chocolate chips

Mix all dry ingredients except chips. Add melted butter. Mix well. Place in two cake pans and bake for 30 minutes at 400°. Stir often to keep from getting lumpy. Add chocolate chips after cereal is cooled. Very delicious and nutritious! We prefer it without chocolate chips.

Mrs. Dewayne (Edna Sue) Miller

Granola

14 c. quick oatmeal
4 c. unsweetened coconut
2 tsp. salt

2 c. brown sugar
1½ c. melted butter

Mix together well. Spread on cookie sheets and toast in oven at 275-300° until brown. Stir often. After cooled, pour into airtight container.

Mrs. Omer (Martha) Miller

Freedom is not the right to do what we want, but the power to do what we ought.

Granola

14 c. oatmeal	2½ c. brown sugar
4 c. coconut	2 c. melted margarine
2 tsp. salt	

Mix and spread on cookie sheets to toast. Bake at approximately 250°.

Mrs. Kenneth (Martha) Miller
Mrs. Alva (Elnora) Hochstetler

Peanut Butter Granola

10 c. oatmeal	3 sticks margarine
1 c. coconut	1 tsp. salt
1 c. sunflower seeds	2 c. brown sugar
1 c. slivered almonds	3 c. peanut butter
1 c. wheat germ	

Melt together margarine, salt, brown sugar, and peanut butter, then mix with the rest. Put in pans and heat in 270° oven until golden brown. Stir a few times while browning.

Mrs. Ernest (Sara) Schrock

Grapenuts

2 c. brown sugar	2 tsp. soda
1 c. molasses	2 tsp. salt
4 c. sour cream (part sour milk	1 tsp. maple flavoring
or buttermilk may be used)	8 c. whole wheat flour

Mix ingredients in order given. Spread on greased cookie sheet and bake at 325° for approximately 45-50 minutes. Cool, then rub through a wire mesh. Spread crumbs on cookie sheets and dry in a warm oven.

Mrs. Stephen (Amelia) Miller

Those that suffer vain worldly thoughts to lodge within them when they are at their devotions, turn the house of prayer into a house of merchandise.

Matthew Henry

Grapenuts

14 c. whole wheat flour
4 c. brown sugar
4 tsp. salt
4 tsp. baking soda

4½ c. sour milk
2 c. melted margarine
2 tsp. maple flavor (or vanilla)

Mix all ingredients together. Put on cookie sheets and bake at 350°. Put through Salad Master, food processor, or grapenut screen and toast at 250°.

Mrs. Kenneth (Martha) Miller

Baked Oatmeal

2 eggs, beaten
1 c. milk
½ c. vegetable oil
1 tsp. salt

1 c. brown sugar
2 tsp. baking powder
3 c. oatmeal

Mix together first 6 ingredients, then stir in oatmeal. Pour into 8 x 12-inch pan. Bake at 350° for 25 minutes. Serve warm with milk.

Alma Bontrager

7-Grain Porridge

1½ c. 7-Grain cereal
3 c. water
¼ c. raisins
¼ c. sliced apples
¼ c. almonds or sunflower seeds

¼ c. brown sugar
½ tsp. cinnamon
¼ tsp. nutmeg
dash of salt

Mix all ingredients in saucepan. Cook on low heat until desired consistency.

Mrs. Stephen (Amelia) Miller

"I will lift up mine eyes unto the hills, from whence cometh my help. My help cometh from the LORD, which made heaven and earth." Psalm 121:1-2

The Easter Story

Long ago when Jesus lived,
Men despised him very much,
So they nailed him to a cross;
Is anything as cruel as such?

Loving hands laid him away,
Into Joseph's rich new tomb.
Now the blessed Saviour's gone;
Was there ever so much gloom?

Jesus rose on the third day,
He had power o'er the dead,
Scared the men who tried to steal
His disciples from the stead.

After forty days from then,
He ascended to the sky,
Disappeared behind a cloud,
His disciples thought, "Oh, why?"

Suddenly they realized
Angels were there by their side,
Saying, "He will come again,
Be your comforter and guide!"

Composed by Deborah Slabaugh

Pies

Sweet Hour of Prayer

My heart said unto thee, Thy face, LORD, will I seek. —Psalm 27:8

William W. Walford, 1772-1850   William B. Bradbury, 1816-1868

1. Sweet hour of prayer, sweet hour of prayer, That calls me from a world of care,
2. Sweet hour of prayer, sweet hour of prayer, Thy wings shall my pe - ti - tion bear
3. Sweet hour of prayer, sweet hour of prayer, May I thy con - so - la - tion share,

And bids me, at my Father's throne, Make all my wants and wish-es known!
To Him, whose truth and faith-ful-ness En - gage the wait - ing soul to bless:
Till, from Mount Pisgah's loft-y height, I view my home, and take my flight:

In sea - sons of dis - tress and grief, My soul has oft - en found re - lief,
And since He bids me seek His face, Be - lieve His Word, and trust His grace,
This robe of flesh I'll drop, and rise, To seize the ev - er - last - ing prize;

And oft es-caped the tempter's snare, By thy re - turn, sweet hour of prayer.
I'll cast on Him my ev - 'ry care, And wait for thee, sweet hour of prayer.
And shout, while passing thro' the air, Farewell, farewell, sweet hour of prayer.

Pie Dough

1 lb. vegetable shortening
1¼ qt. flour

½ T. salt
1 c. warm water

Mix all together at one time.

Mrs. John (Carolyn) Otto

Thank-You Pie Filling

1 gal. water
1 lb. margarine
4½ c. sugar
4½ c. brown sugar
3 c. water
3 c. Perma-flo

1 T. vanilla
½ tsp. salt
2 T. lemon juice
apples, sliced
cinnamon

Heat water, margarine, and sugar. Mix Perma-flo and stir in and boil a few minutes. Add vanilla and salt; stir well. Add lemon juice, apples, and cinnamon.

Mrs. Ernest (Mary Ellen) Miller

Cherry Pie Filling

5 qt. sour cherries, pitted
1 qt. water
4 to 6 T. margarine
4 to 5 c. sugar

pinch salt
1½ c. ThermFlo
3 c. water
almond flavoring

Drain juice from cherries into 13 qt. bowl or kettle. Add water, margarine, sugar, and salt. Heat to boiling point, then add ThermFlo and cherries. Stir well, and boil a few minutes. Add almond flavor and cherries.

Mrs. Ernest (Mary Ellen) Miller

Remember, you are not only the salt of the earth, but the sugar.

Raisin Pie Filling

2 qt. water
3 c. sugar
1½ sticks margarine
6 c. raisins*

salt
vanilla
1 c. ThermFlo
2 c. water

Bring to a boil the first 5 ingredients; thicken with ThermFlo and water. Add vanilla. Bake with crust on top. *I usually boil the raisins 5-10 minutes.

Mrs. Ernest (Mary Ellen) Miller

Grandma's Lemon Pie

1¼ c. sugar
6 T. cornstarch
2 c. water
3 egg yolks
  Meringue:
½ c. plus 2 T. water
1 T. cornstarch
3 egg whites

3 T. butter or margarine
⅓ c. lemon juice
2 tsp. vinegar
1½ tsp. lemon extract

6 T. sugar
1 tsp. vanilla
pinch salt

In a saucepan, combine sugar and cornstarch. Gradually add water. Cook and stir over medium-high heat until thickened and bubbly. Reduce heat to low; cook and stir for 2 minutes. Remove from heat. Stir 1 c. of hot filling into egg yolks. Return all to pan and bring to a gentle boil. Cook for 2 minutes, stirring constantly. Remove from heat. Stir in butter. Gently stir in lemon juice, vinegar, and extract. Pour hot filling into baked crust. For meringue, combine water and cornstarch in a saucepan until smooth. Cook and stir until thickened and clear, about 2 minutes. Cool completely. Meanwhile, beat egg whites in a mixing bowl until foamy. Gradually beat in sugar until stiff peaks form. Beat in vanilla and salt. Gradually add cornstarch mixture, beating well. Immediately spread over warm filling, sealing edges to crust. Bake at 350° for 10-12 minutes or until meringue is golden brown. Cool. Store in the refrigerator. Makes 1 pie.

Mrs. Jerome (Rose) Graber

God wants our precious
time, not our spare time.

Pear Pie

4 medium pears, chopped
juice of ½ lemon
1 c. sugar
¼ c. flour
3 eggs

⅛ tsp. salt
¼ c. butter
¼ c. cream
cinnamon

Spread pears in a 9-inch pastry shell. Sprinkle with lemon juice. Mix together rest of ingredients and pour over pears. Sprinkle with cinnamon. Bake at 350° for 45 minutes or until browned and set like custard. Serves 6-8.

Mrs. Stephen (Amelia) Miller

Pineapple Pie

1 9-inch graham cracker crust
1 c. milk
½ lb. marshmallows
2 T. lemon Jell-O

1 20-oz. can drained crushed
  pineapple
1 c. whipped cream (unsweetened)

In a saucepan heat milk, marshmallows, and gelatin until marshmallows are melted. Cool. Add pineapple and whipped cream. Fold all together; pour into graham cracker crust. Refrigerate 4-5 hours. Serves 6.

Mrs. Omer (Martha) Miller

Fluffy Cranberry Cheese Pie

Cranberry topping:
1 3-oz. pkg. raspberry Jell-O
⅓ c. sugar
Filling:
1 3-oz. pkg. cream cheese,
  softened
¼ c. sugar
1 T. milk

1¼ c. cranberry juice
1 8-oz. can jellied cranberry sauce

1 tsp. vanilla
½ c. frozen whipped topping,
  thawed
1 9-inch pastry shell, baked

In a mixing bowl, combine gelatin and sugar; set aside. In a saucepan, bring cranberry juice to a boil. Remove from heat and pour over gelatin mixture, stirring to dissolve. Stir in the cranberry sauce. Chill until slightly thickened. Meanwhile, in another mixing bowl, beat cream cheese, sugar, milk, and vanilla until fluffy. Fold in the whipped topping. Spread evenly into pie shell. Beat cranberry topping until frothy; pour over filling. Chill overnight. Serves 6-8.

Mrs. Wilbur (Joann) Hochstetler

Chocolate Chiffon Pie

2 T. gelatin
½ c. cold water
1½ c. sugar
¼ tsp. salt
2½ c. milk

4 T. cocoa
2 tsp. instant coffee
2 c. whipped cream
2 tsp. vanilla

Dissolve gelatin in cold water. Mix sugar, salt, milk, cocoa, and coffee in sauce-pan. Bring to a boil, then add gelatin. Cool until it thickens. Add whipped cream and vanilla. Put in crusts and chill! (Double recipe for 5 pies.)

Mrs. James (Rosanna) Miller

Chocolate Chip Pie

3 c. sugar
1 qt. milk
6 egg yolks
½ c. cold water

3 T. gelatin
1 tsp. vanilla
1 pt. whipped topping
  grated chocolate chips

Cook sugar, egg yolks, and milk together in double boiler ½ hour (do not boil). Pour hot over gelatin dissolved in cold water. Cool until slightly jelled, then add the whipped topping and vanilla. Divide into 2 baked pie shells and sprinkle with grated chocolate chips. Makes 2 pies.

Mrs. Wilmer (Clara Mae) Yoder

Creamy Chocolate Crackle Pie

1 5-oz. Crackle candy bar
1 8-oz. carton whipped dessert topping

1 graham cracker pie shell

Melt candy bar in the top of a double boiler. Blend with whipped topping. Turn into pie shell and place in freezer for 2 hours.

Kathryn Mary Kauffman

A man should never be ashamed to own that he has been wrong, which is but saying in other words that he is wiser today than he was yesterday.
Alexander Pope

Wet Bottom Shoo-Fly Pie

Crumbs:

6 c. flour	1 c. shortening
2 c. brown sugar	1 tsp. baking soda

Liquid:

3 c. molasses (golden)	½ c. sugar
3 c. hot water	½ c. brown sugar
1 tsp. baking soda	3 eggs, beaten

Crumbs: Combine all ingredients; mix well. Reserve 3 c. crumbs to mix with liquid.

Liquid: Combine molasses, water, soda, brown sugar, sugar, and eggs; add reserved crumbs; mix well. Pour into 5 or 6 unbaked pie shells. Top with remaining crumbs. Bake at 425° for 10 minutes, then at 350° for 45 minutes.

Mrs. Ben (Anna Mary) Fisher

Sadie Glick's Shoo-Fly Pie

Liquid:	*Crumbs:*
4 eggs	3 c. dark brown sugar
½ c. dark brown sugar	6 scant c. all-purpose flour
2 c. King syrup (I use fresh	½ tsp. salt
sorghum molasses)	1 tsp. baking soda
2 c. boiling water	½ c. lard (heaping)
1 tsp. baking soda	

For liquid: Lightly mix eggs and sugar. Add syrup and stir until smooth before adding boiling water and soda. Stir well and set aside.

For crumbs: Mix together; add 2 double handfuls of crumbs to liquid and fold in lightly. Divide into 4 8-inch pie shells. Spread rest of crumbs over top. Bake at 300° approximately 50-55 minutes.

Note: If pies are not rising after 40 minutes in oven, your oven needs to be hotter.

Mrs. Stephen (Amelia) Miller

Begin each morning
with a talk with God.

Caramel Pie

¾ c. sugar (½ brown)
1 rounded T. flour
2 c. milk, half cream

2 eggs, separated
½ tsp. maple flavoring
pinch of salt

Mix flour, sugar, egg yolks, and salt. Add enough milk to make paste. Scald the remaining milk. Beat egg whites and add flavoring. Add milk and egg whites to other ingredients. Pour into pie pan, sprinkle nuts on top. Bake at 375° for 35-45 minutes or until done. Serves 6-7.

Ruby Chupp

Maple Pie

1 c. maple syrup
4 beaten eggs
½ c. sugar

⅓ c. melted margarine
1 c. walnuts
dash of salt

Combine all ingredients and put in unbaked pie shell. Bake at 350° for 35 minutes. Serves 6-8.

Mrs. John (Fannie) Miller

Oatmeal Pie

¾ c. sugar
¼ c. maple syrup
¾ c. corn syrup
4 eggs, beaten

½ tsp. salt
⅓ c. milk
1 tsp. vanilla
¾ c. oatmeal

Blend all ingredients together and pour into 9-inch pastry-lined pie plate. Bake at 350° for 1 hour or until golden and just set. Serves 6-7.

Ruby Chupp

The encouraging words DO NOT FEAR are found 366 times in the Bible. Once for each day, even when it's leap year.

The Authentic Amish Cookbook

Oatmeal Pie

1 c. brown sugar
1 c. light syrup
¾ c. oatmeal
4 eggs

¼ tsp. salt
1 tsp. vanilla
⅓ c. water

Beat eggs and then add the rest of ingredients and beat well. Pour into unbaked pie shells and bake at 350° for about 45 minutes. The middle will appear soft.

Mrs. Ernest (Sara) Schrock

Pumpkin Pie

¾ c. pumpkin
1 rounded T. flour
½ c. sugar
½ c. brown sugar
¼ tsp. salt

2 eggs, separated
1 tsp. cinnamon
1 tsp. pumpkin pie spice
2 c. milk (half canned milk or cream)

Mix the sugar and flour; add to the pumpkin. Add the egg yolks, spices, and milk. Fold in beaten egg whites last. Bake at 450° for 10 minutes, then at 350° until set.

Ruby W. Mast

Pumpkin Pie

8 eggs
10 c. pumpkin
5⅓ c. sugar
2 tsp. salt

6 tsp. cinnamon
1 T. cloves
10 c. milk

Beat eggs, add sugar, pumpkin, salt, spices, and milk, then beat again. Bake at 350° until set. Makes 8-9 pies.

Mrs. Dan (Mary) Miller

Kind words are jewels that live in the heart and soul and remain as blessed memories years after they have been spoken.
Marrea Johnson

Layer Pumpkin Pie

4 oz. cream cheese
1 T. milk
1 T. sugar
1½ c. Cool Whip
1 graham cracker crust
1 c. milk

1 16-oz. can pumpkin
2 3-oz. pkg. vanilla instant pudding
1 tsp. cinnamon
½ tsp. ginger
¼ tsp. cloves

In a large bowl, mix cream cheese, 1 T. milk, and sugar with wire whisk until smooth. Gently stir in whipped topping. Spread on bottom of pie crust. Into a large bowl, pour 1 c. milk. Add pumpkin, pudding, and spices. Whisk together until well blended (mixture will be thick). Spread over cream cheese layer. Refrigerate 4 hours. Garnish with Cool Whip if desired.

Mrs. Orlie (Mary) Troyer

Libby's Pumpkin Pie

2 eggs
1½ c. Libby's canned pumpkin
¾ c. sugar
½ tsp. salt
1 tsp. cinnamon

½ tsp. ginger
¼ tsp. cloves
1⅔ c. evaporated milk or
    light cream

Beat the eggs slightly. Mix filling ingredients in order given. Pour into 9-inch pie shell. Bake in preheated oven at 425° for 15 minutes. Reduce temperature to 350° and bake 45 minutes or until knife inserted in center of pie filling comes out clean. Cool. Garnish with whipped cream if desired. Makes 1 9-inch pie.

Mrs. John Almon Mast

Begin each new day as if it were the beginning of your life, for truly it is the beginning of the rest of your life.

Pumpkin Custard Pie

1 c. pumpkin or squash
3 eggs, separated
1 T. flour
¼ c. brown sugar
½ c. white sugar

½ tsp. salt
½ tsp. cinnamon
¾ tsp. pumpkin pie spice
2 c. milk, scalded

Mix ingredients in order given, folding in beaten egg whites last. Pour into unbaked pie shell and bake at 450° for 5 minutes, then at 325° for 40 minutes or until done.

Beth Ann Yoder

Custard Pie

4 or 5 eggs, separated
1½ c. sugar

2 T. flour
3½ c. boiling milk

Beat yolks and whites separately, then beat together. Add sugar and flour. Mix well, then add hot milk. Beat all together with egg beater. Put in oven while mixture is hot. Sprinkle with cinnamon. Bake in low heat oven at 275°. (Takes about 1 hour.)

Mrs. John (Carolyn) Otto

Custard Pie

1 can evaporated milk
1 c. regular milk
3 eggs, separated
½ c. white sugar

½ c. brown sugar
dash of salt
1 tsp. vanilla

Preheat oven to 425°. Scald the milk. Beat the egg whites. Mix together the egg yolks, sugar, salt, and vanilla. Add the milk. Fold in the egg whites last. Bake at 425° until the top is brown, then reduce to 200° until set.

Ruby W. Mast

How do you sleep at night? Do you count sheep or talk to the Shepherd?

Rhubarb Cream Pie

1 c. cream	1 egg
1 c. sugar	1 tsp. vanilla
1 T. cornstarch	pinch of salt

Mix and add 2 c. chopped rhubarb. Bake in unbaked pie crust.

Beth Ann Yoder

Raisin Cream Pie

2 c. water	2 egg yolks
¼ c. white sugar	⅛ tsp. salt
½ c. brown sugar	½ c. raisins
½ c. cream	1 tsp. vanilla
3 T. ThermFlo	1 T. butter

Simmer water and raisins for 5-10 minutes. Mix sugars, cream, ThermFlo, egg yolks, and salt. Add to water and raisins. Cook until thickened. Add vanilla and butter. Cool. Put in baked crust; top with whipped topping.

Mrs. Perry (Delores) Herschberger

Recipe for Life

1 c. good thoughts	2 c. well-beaten faults
1 c. kind deeds	3 c. forgiveness
1 c. consideration of others	

Mix thoroughly and add tears of joy, sorrow, and sympathy for others. Fold in 4 cups prayer and faith to lighten other ingredients and let rise to great heights of Christian living. After pouring all this into your family life, bake well with the warmth of human kindness. Serve with a smile.

Mrs. Michael (Lydia Ann) Stoll

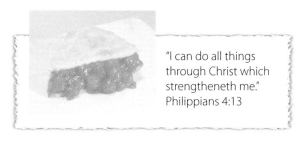

"I can do all things through Christ which strengtheneth me."
Philippians 4:13

Little Girl Pies

1 c. sugar
½ c. shortening
1 egg
½ c. milk
   Filling:
½ c. sugar
1 T. cornstarch

1 tsp. vanilla
3½ c. all-purpose flour
½ tsp. salt
4 tsp. baking powder

½ c. water
1 c. raisins

Cream sugar and shortening. Add egg, milk, and vanilla; mix well. Combine dry ingredients; add to creamed mixture and beat well. Chill. Meanwhile, for filling combine sugar and cornstarch in a saucepan. Add water and stir to dissolve. Add raisins and cook until mixture is thick, stirring constantly. Set aside to cool. Roll chilled dough on floured board to ⅛-inch thickness. Cut into 3-inch circles. Use a thimble to cut small holes in the center of ½ of the circles. Place 1 tsp. filling on solid circles; top with a circle that has a hole. Press edges together firmly. Bake at 375° for 15-17 minutes on greased sheets. Yields 2 dozen.

Mrs. Michael (Lydia Ann) Stoll

When God measures a man,
He puts the tape
around the heart,
not the head.

Ten Ways to Help Mother

1. Look pleasant.

2. Speak softly and kindly.

3. Do your work cheerfully and well.

4. Do not wait to be told every little duty, but surprise her by doing things she has not told you to do.

5. See how many times you can save her steps by running errands.

6. Put your cap, coat, and schoolbooks in their proper places. Then you will not need to trouble her to help you find them and the home will look more tidy.

7. Let her know that you are thankful for what she does for you.

8. Notice when she is tired or is not feeling well or has a headache and be quiet.

9. Say to her sometimes, "I love you."

10. Pray for her.

If you follow these suggestions, there will be at least two happy persons—you and your mother. Try it and see!

Cakes, Cookies, and Frostings

Amazing Grace

That . . . he might shew the exceeding riches of his grace. —Ephesians 2:7

John Newton, 1725-1807   Early American Melody

1. A - maz - ing grace! how sweet the sound That saved a wretch like me!
2. 'Twas grace that taught my heart to fear, And grace my fears re-lieved;
3. Thro' man - y dan-gers, toils and snares, I have al - read - y come;
4. The Lord has prom - ised good to me, His word my hope se-cures;
5. When we've been there ten thousand years, Bright shin-ing as the sun;

I once was lost, but now I'm found, Was blind, but now I see.
How pre - cious did that grace ap - pear The hour I first be-lieved.
'Twas grace that bro't me safe thus far And grace will lead me home.
He will my shield and por - tion be As long as life en-dures.
We've no less days to sing God's praise Than when we first be-gun.

Apple Cake

4 c. apples, chopped
½ c. vegetable oil
2 c. sugar
2 eggs, beaten
2 c. flour
½ tsp. salt
1½ tsp. baking soda
1½ tsp. cinnamon

1 tsp. vanilla
1 c. raisins or chopped nuts
Topping:
¼ c. sugar
½ c. brown sugar
½ tsp. cinnamon
½ c. chopped nuts

Combine apples, oil, and sugar. Add eggs. Sift together flour, soda, salt, and cinnamon and add to batter. Stir in vanilla and nuts. Bake in greased 9 x 13-inch pan in 350° oven for 45 minutes or until done.

Before baking, crumble together the four topping ingredients and sprinkle on batter. When done baking, cool slightly and glaze with a powdered sugar glaze. Enjoy!

Mrs. Marcus (Mary) Gingerich

Apple Cake

4 c. diced apples
2 c. sugar
1 egg
2 c. flour
Hot Sauce:
1 c. brown sugar
1 c. white sugar

2 tsp. cinnamon
2 tsp. baking soda
1 c. chopped nuts

2 c. water
4 T. flour

Combine apples and sugar and let stand until sugar dissolves. Add egg and beat. Stir in dry ingredients. Pour into 13 x 9 x 2-inch baking pan. Cook sauce until clear, then add ½ c. butter and 2 tsp. vanilla, and pour over cake while sauce is still hot. Bake at 375° for 35-40 minutes.

Mrs. Joe (Susie) Delagrange

Holding on to anger is like grasping a hot coal with the intent of throwing it at someone else—you are the one who gets burned!
Buddha

. . .

Love never asks how much must I do; but how much can I do?
Frederick A. Agar

Apple Dapple Cake

2 eggs
2 c. white sugar
1 c. vegetable oil
3 c. flour (scant)
½ tsp. salt
  Icing:
1 c. brown sugar

1 tsp. baking soda
3 c. chopped apples
2 tsp. vanilla
nuts, optional

¼ c. milk
¼ c. margarine

Mix eggs, sugar, and oil. Add sifted dry ingredients, then add apples, nuts, and vanilla. Bake at 350° for 45 minutes or until done.

Icing: Cook 2½ minutes. Stir a little after removing from stove, then pour over cake while still hot.

Ruby Chupp

Banana Cake

1 c. white sugar
4 T. butter
2 eggs, separated
3½ c. mashed bananas

1½ c. flour
¼ tsp. salt
1 tsp. baking soda
nuts

Cream butter and sugar; add egg yolks, bananas, soda, and salt; beat well. Add flour and nuts. Beat egg whites until peaks form and fold in last. Bake in a 9 x 13-inch pan at 350° for 45 minutes.

Mrs. Michael (Lydia Ann) Stoll

Banana Nut Cake

5 c. flour
2½ tsp. baking powder
2½ tsp. soda
2 tsp. salt
3⅓ c. sugar
1⅓ c. shortening

6 eggs
2½ c. mashed bananas
2 c. milk made sour
  with 2 T. vinegar
1⅓ c. nuts

Mix well and bake in 11 x 17 x 2-inch cake pan at 350°.

Mrs. Perry (Delores) Herschberger

Blueberry Crunch Cake

½ c. margarine
¾ c. sugar
2 eggs
⅓ c. milk
1 tsp. vanilla

2 c. flour
2 tsp. baking powder
½ tsp. salt
1 qt. blueberry pie filling

Cream margarine and sugar; beat in eggs; add milk and vanilla; add sifted dry ingredients. Spread ½ of batter in 9 x 9-inch pan. Cover with ½ of blueberry pie filling; spread remaining batter then remaining filling. Mix ½ c. sugar and ½ c. flour. Cut in 2 T. margarine; sprinkle on top. Bake at 350° for 45 minutes or until done.

Mrs. Joe (Susie) Delagrange

Pineapple Sheet Cake

⅔ c. warm milk
2 tsp. sugar
1 T. yeast
3 egg yolks

3 c. flour
½ lb. margarine
2 cans crushed pineapple

Put yeast in warm milk and sugar. Then add beaten egg yolks, flour, and margarine. Work like roll dough. Roll out dough. Put half of dough in bottom of cake pan. Pour on crushed pineapple. Put rest of rolled out dough on top. Let set 1 hour. Bake 30 minutes. Frost with thin powdered sugar frosting.

Mrs. David (Rhoda) Miller

Pineapple Sheet Cake

2 c. sugar
2 c. flour
2 eggs

2 tsp. baking powder
1 tsp. baking soda
1 can crushed pineapple

Mix well. Bake at 350° for 20 minutes or until golden brown. Bake on cookie sheet. Frost with cream cheese frosting and put nuts on top. Serves 24.

Miriam Miller

Truth is not popular,
but it is always right.

Upside-Down Cake

1 c. cake flour
2 eggs, separated
1 T. butter
1 c. sugar

1 tsp. baking powder
1 tsp. vanilla
¼ tsp. salt
6 T. milk or fruit juice

Cover bottom of 9 x 13-inch cake pan with fruit of your choice. (If not sweetened, sprinkle with sugar.) Mix all ingredients together, adding beaten egg whites last. Bake at 350° until golden or until a toothpick comes out clean. Serve warm with milk.

Mrs. Loyal (Dorcas) Gingerich

Cherry Fruitcake

3 c. all-purpose flour
2 c. sugar
2 tsp. baking powder
2 tsp. salt
2 lb. pitted dates
2 lb. diced, candied pineapple

4 lb. red maraschino cherries,
   drained
3 lb. pecan halves
12 eggs
⅔ c. orange juice

Grease pans and line with greased waxed paper. Sift dry ingredients. Add fruits and pecans; toss until coated. Beat eggs and orange juice together and pour over fruit mixture. Toss until completely combined. Pour mixture into prepared pans, pressing with spatula to pack tightly. Bake at 250° for 1½ to 1¾ hours or until toothpick comes out clean. Allow cakes to cool in pans 10 minutes. Remove from pans, tear off paper, and brush with light corn syrup while still warm. Cool thoroughly.

Beth Ann Yoder

Help us, O God, to treat every human heart as if it were breaking and to consider the feelings of others as we do our own.

. . .

Anxiety does not empty tomorrow of its trials. It simply empties today of its joys.

. . .

Let not your heart be troubled; the Lord will see you through.

Cherry Cake

1 20-oz. can cherry pie filling
1 20-oz. can crushed pineapple,
  with juice
1 box yellow cake mix

1 c. melted butter
1 c. unsweetened coconut
1 c. nuts

Spread pie filling in bottom of 9 x 13-inch cake pan. Cover with pineapple. Sprinkle dry cake mix over top and pour melted butter over all. Sprinkle coconut and nuts on top. Serve warm with ice cream.

Mrs. Omer (Martha) Miller

Lemon Meringue Cake

1 box lemon or yellow cake mix
1 c. water
  Filling:
1 c. sugar
3 T. cornstarch
¼ tsp. salt
½ c. water
  Meringue:
4 egg whites
¼ tsp. cream of tartar

3 eggs
⅓ c. vegetable oil

¼ c. lemon juice
4 egg yolks, beaten
4 tsp. butter
1 tsp. grated lemon peel

¾ c. sugar

In a mixing bowl, combine cake mix, eggs, water, and oil. Beat until blended. Pour into two greased and floured round baking pans. Bake at 350° for 25-30 minutes. Cool for 10 minutes; remove from pans to wire racks. For filling, combine sugar, cornstarch, and salt in a saucepan. Stir in water and juice until smooth. Bring to a boil over medium heat; cook and stir 1-2 minutes or until thickened. Remove from heat. Stir a small amount of hot filling into egg yolks; return to pan, stirring constantly. Bring to a gentle boil; cook and stir for 2 minutes. Remove from heat; stir in butter and lemon peel. Cool completely. For meringue, in a mixing bowl, beat egg whites and cream of tartar until foamy. Gradually beat in sugar until stiff peaks form. To assemble, split each cake into 2 layers. Place bottom layer on an ovenproof plate; spread with a third of the filling. Repeat layers twice. Top with fourth cake layer. Spread meringue over top and sides; bake at 350° for 10-15 minutes or until meringue is lightly browned. Refrigerate. Serves 12-14.

Martha Graber

Lemon Chiffon Cake

2 eggs, separated
1½ c. sugar
2¼ c. sifted flour
3 tsp. baking powder
1 tsp. salt

⅓ c. cooking oil
1 c. milk
2 tsp. lemon juice
grated rind of 1 lemon (if desired)

Sift 1 c. sugar with flour, baking powder, and salt. Add the oil, half of milk, and lemon juice and rind. Beat until fluffy, then add egg yolks and remaining milk, beating until smooth. Beat egg whites until frothy; gradually beat in ½ cup of the sugar, beating until stiff and glossy. Fold this into the batter. Bake at 350° for 30 minutes.

Mary Ann Mast

Raisin Delicious

First part:
1 c. packed brown sugar
3 c. boiling water
1 c. white sugar
2 T. butter
   Cake part:
2¼ c. all-purpose flour
1 c. white sugar
3 T. butter

½ tsp. salt
1½ c. raisins
½ tsp. cinnamon

3¾ tsp. baking powder
¾ tsp. salt
1 c. milk
3 tsp. vanilla

Pour cake part into 13 x 9 x 2-inch pan. Boil first part 15 minutes. Pour over cake part and bake.

Mrs. Joe (Susie) Delagrange

Pumpkin Cake

1 box yellow or white cake mix
1 pkg. instant butterscotch pudding
4 eggs
¼ c. water

¼ c. oil
1 c. pumpkin
2 tsp. pumpkin pie spice

Beat 5 minutes; bake in tube pan 1 hour at 350°. Very moist and good. Frost with Wanda's Frosting (page 82).

Lena Yoder

Pumpkin Bundt Cake

1 18¼-oz. pkg. yellow cake mix
1 3.4-oz. pkg. instant butterscotch
   pudding mix
4 eggs
¼ c. water
¼ c. vegetable oil
1 c. canned pumpkin
2 tsp. pumpkin pie spice
whipped cream, optional

In a large mixing bowl, combine the first 7 ingredients. Beat on low speed for 30 seconds; beat on medium for 4 minutes. Pour into a greased and floured 10-inch fluted tube pan. Bake at 350° for 50-55 minutes or until a toothpick inserted near the center comes out clean. Cool in pan for 15 minutes before removing to a wire rack to cool completely. Serve with whipped cream if desired. Serves 16.

Amy Elizabeth Kauffman

Carrot Cake

3 eggs
2 c. sugar
1½ c. oil
3 c. grated carrots
2 tsp. vanilla
1 tsp. baking powder
¾ c. nuts
3 c. flour
½ tsp. salt
½ tsp. cinnamon
1 tsp. baking soda
¼ tsp. nutmeg
1 c. crushed pineapple, undrained
   Frosting:
8 oz. cream cheese
1 stick margarine
about 1 lb. powdered sugar
vanilla

Beat eggs; add sugar and oil, then remaining ingredients. Add carrots last. Pour in 9 x 13-inch cake pan and bake at 350°. Frost when cooled.

Regina Miller

Snowflakes are one of nature's most fragile things, but just look at what they can do when they stick together.

Vera M. Kelly

. . .

How beautiful a day can be when touched by love.

Oatmeal Cake

1 c. oatmeal	1½ c. flour
1½ c. boiling water	2 eggs
½ c. margarine or	1 tsp. salt
liquid shortening	1 tsp. cinnamon
1 c. brown sugar	1½ tsp. baking soda
1 c. white sugar	1 tsp. vanilla

Mix first 2 ingredients. Set aside. Cream margarine and sugars. Mix remaining ingredients. Now put all together. Bake in greased loaf pan at 350° for 40 minutes or until finished.

Mrs. Earl (Irma) Chupp

Lazy Daisy Oatmeal Cake

1¼ c. boiling water	2 eggs
1 c. quick oats	1½ c. flour
½ c. butter	1 tsp. baking soda
1 c. sugar	½ tsp. salt
1 c. brown sugar, firmly packed	¾ tsp. cinnamon
1 tsp. vanilla	¼ tsp. nutmeg

Pour water over oats; cover and let stand 20 minutes. Cream butter, sugar, and brown sugar; beat until fluffy. Blend in vanilla, eggs, and oats mixture. Mix well. Combine flour, soda, salt, cinnamon, and nutmeg and blend into mixture. Put in greased and floured 9-inch square pan. Bake 50-55 minutes at 350°.

Mrs. Ben (Anna Mary) Fisher

Oatmeal Chocolate Cake

1¾ c. boiling water	1¾ c. flour
1 c. uncooked oatmeal	1 tsp. baking soda
1 c. brown sugar	½ tsp. salt
1 c. white sugar	1 T. cocoa
½ c. butter	1 12-oz. pkg. (2 c.) chocolate chips
2 large eggs	¾ c. nuts

Pour boiling water over oatmeal. Let stand 10 minutes. Add sugar and butter. Stir until butter is melted; add rest of ingredients, except half of chocolate chips and nuts. Pour in greased 9 x 13-inch pan. Sprinkle nuts and rest of chocolate chips on top. Bake at 350° about 40 minutes. Very good.

Mrs. Edna Slabaugh

Ann's Chocolate Cake

¾ c. cocoa
1½ c. boiling water
¾ c. margarine or shortening
1½ c. sugar
3 eggs

2¼ c. flour
1½ tsp. baking powder
1½ tsp. baking soda
¾ tsp. salt
1½ tsp. vanilla

In a small bowl, pour boiling water over cocoa. Stir until dissolved; set aside. Cream together margarine and sugar; add eggs and vanilla. Mix well. Add dry ingredients to creamed mixture alternately with cocoa mixture. Put in greased 9 x 13-inch pan. Bake at 350° for 30 minutes or until toothpick inserted in center comes out clean.

Mrs. John (Fannie) Miller

Miracle Whip Cake

2 c. flour
1 c. sugar
2 tsp. baking soda
4 T. cocoa
½ tsp. salt

1 scant cup Miracle Whip
    dressing
1 c. cold water
1 tsp. vanilla

Mix first five ingredients together; add remaining ones. Bake at 350° for 25-30 minutes in a sheet cake pan. For a quick and easy cake, this is next to a cake mix.

Mrs. David (Rhoda) Miller

Quick and Easy Chocolate Cake

3 c. flour
1¾ c. sugar
2 tsp. salt
2 tsp. baking soda
5 T. cocoa powder

1 c. vegetable oil
2 T. vinegar
1 T. vanilla
2 c. cold water

Mix in order given. Bake at 350° for 30 minutes.

Mrs. Nathan (Mattie) Miller

Texas Sheet Cake

2 c. flour
2 c. sugar
½ c. cocoa
1 c. shortening
1 c. water
   Frosting:
¼ c. shortening
½ c. cocoa
1 tsp. vanilla

2 eggs, beaten
½ c. sour milk
1 tsp. baking soda
1 tsp. vanilla

6 T. milk
3 c. powdered sugar
½ c. chopped nuts
   or coconut

Bring to boil the cocoa, water, and shortening. Mix with flour and sugar. Add eggs. Mix sour milk and soda, then add to the batter. Add vanilla. Bake on cookie sheet at 350° for 20 minutes or until done. Mix together frosting ingredients. Spread frosting on cake while cake is hot.

Mrs. Ernest (Sara) Schrock

Toffee-Mocha Cream Torte

1 c. butter or margarine, softened
2 c. sugar
2 eggs
1½ tsp. vanilla
2⅔ c. flour
¾ c. cocoa
   Topping:
½ tsp. instant coffee granules
1 tsp. hot water
2 c. whipping cream

2 tsp. baking soda
¼ tsp. salt
1 c. buttermilk
2 tsp. instant coffee granules
1 c. boiling water

3 T. brown sugar
6 1.4-oz. Heath candy bars,
   crushed and divided

In mixing bowl, cream butter and sugar. Beat in eggs and vanilla. Combine the flour, cocoa, baking soda, and salt; add to creamed mixture alternately with the buttermilk. Dissolve coffee in water; add to batter. Beat for 2 minutes. Pour into 3 greased and floured 9-inch round pans. Bake at 350° for 16-20 minutes or until done. Cool for 10 minutes before removing from pans to wire racks to cool completely. For topping, dissolve coffee in water in a mixing bowl; cool. Add cream and brown sugar. Beat until stiff peaks form. Place bottom cake layer on a serving plate; top with 1⅓ c. of topping. Sprinkle with ½ c. of crushed candy bars. Repeat layers twice. Store in the refrigerator. Serves 12-14.

Mrs. Norman (Marlena) Miller

Chocolate Pudding Cake

1 box white cake mix   2 c. milk
1 box instant chocolate pudding   2 egg whites

Place all ingredients in a mixing bowl. Beat well. Bake in a 9 x 13-inch greased cake pan. Bake at 350° for 35-40 minutes.

Mrs. Jerome (Rose) Graber

Supper Cake

½ c. shortening   3 c. flour
1 egg   3 tsp. baking powder
1½ c. sugar   ¼ tsp. salt
1 c. milk   rhubarb, or any fruit

Cut rhubarb fine and put in 9 x 13-inch pan. Sprinkle with 1 c. sugar and dot with butter. Pour batter over top and bake at 350° for 35-45 minutes. Eat with milk.

Mrs. Monroe (Elsie) Miller

Italian Creme Cake

5 egg whites, beaten   1 tsp. baking soda
1 stick margarine   1 c. buttermilk
½ c. shortening   1 tsp. vanilla
2 c. sugar   1 c. nuts, chopped
5 egg yolks   1 c. coconut
2 c. flour
  Icing: ½ c. margarine
8 oz. cream cheese   2¼ c. powdered sugar

Cream margarine, shortening, sugar, and egg yolks. Add rest of ingredients, folding egg whites in last. Bake at 350° in 2 9-inch pans. Cream together icing ingredients and spread on cooled cakes.

Mrs. Noah (Fannie) Yoder

A man who has a thousand friends
Has not one to spare.
He who has an enemy
Meets him everywhere.

Cream Velvet Cake

2½ c. flour
1½ c. sugar
4 tsp. baking powder
½ c. salad oil
1 tsp. salt

1 c. water
4 eggs, divided
2 tsp. vanilla
1 tsp. lemon flavoring
¼ tsp. cream of tartar

Mix together flour, sugar, baking powder, and salt. Make a well and add in order oil, water, egg yolks, vanilla, and lemon flavor; break egg yolks with a spoon and stir into liquid. Continue stirring to mix in dry ingredients. Beat until smooth. Add cream of tartar to egg whites and beat until they form stiff peaks. Gently fold into first mixture. Bake in a quick oven at 350° for 25 minutes or until cake springs back when touched.

Carol Ann Yoder

Red Velvet Cake

2 eggs
1½ c. sugar
½ c. shortening
2 T. baking cocoa
1 tsp. baking soda
1 T. vinegar

1 tsp. vanilla
1½ T. red food coloring
1 c. cake flour
1 c. flour
1 c. buttermilk

Sift together the flours. Cream shortening and sugar. Add eggs. Combine food coloring, baking cocoa, and vanilla. Stir into creamed mixture. Alternately add flour with buttermilk to creamed mixture. Combine soda and vinegar; add to creamed mixture. Mix well. Bake at 350° for 30 minutes or until done. Bake in 2 9-inch pans, then put together as a layer cake.

Mrs. Norman (Marlena) Miller

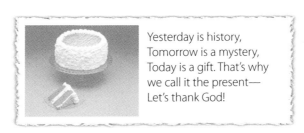

Yesterday is history,
Tomorrow is a mystery,
Today is a gift. That's why
we call it the present—
Let's thank God!

Cream Cheese Sheet Cake

1 c. butter or margarine, softened
8 oz. cream cheese, softened
2 c. sugar
2¼ c. cake flour
   Frosting:
1 c. sugar
⅓ c. milk

6 eggs
¾ tsp. vanilla
1 tsp. baking powder

½ c. butter or margarine
½ c. semisweet chocolate chips

Cream butter, cream cheese, and sugar. Add eggs, one at a time, beating well after each addition. Beat in vanilla. Add baking powder and flour. Pour into a greased 15 x 10 x 1-inch pan. Bake at 325° for 35 minutes or until toothpick inserted near the center comes out clean. Cool completely.

Frosting: Combine sugar and milk in a saucepan; bring to a boil over medium heat. Cover and cook for 3 minutes (do not stir). Stir in butter and chips until melted. Cool slightly and spread over cake. Serves 24.

Mrs. Omer (Martha) Miller

Whipped Cream Cake

1 c. cream
2 eggs
¾ c. sugar
½ tsp. salt

1 tsp. vanilla
1½ c. flour
1 tsp. baking powder
1 tsp. baking soda

Whip cream until stiff. Add eggs one at a time; beat again. Add sugar and vanilla and whip. Sift flour a few times, measure. Add salt, baking powder, and soda, then sift again. Add gradually, beating well. Bake at 350° for 35 minutes.

Marjorie Mast

Easy Dump Cake Dessert

1 21-oz. can cherry pie filling
   (blueberry or strawberry can
   also be used)
1 pkg. yellow cake mix

1 8-oz. can crushed pineapple,
   undrained
½ c. margarine or butter, melted

Heat oven to 350°. Spread pie filling and pineapple in ungreased 13 x 9 x 2-inch cake pan. Stir together dry cake mix and margarine until crumbly. Sprinkle evenly over fruit. Bake for 35-40 minutes or until light brown. Delicious served warm with ice cream or whipped cream.

Mrs. Orlie (Mary) Troyer

Quick Cake

1 No. 2-can cherry pie filling
1 No. 2-can pineapple, crushed
1 box yellow cake mix

1 c. melted butter
1 c. chopped nuts

Pour pie filling into 9 x 13-inch pan and spread. Pour pineapple over cherry filling as is. Spread dry cake mix over pineapple. Spread butter over mixture. Sprinkle with nuts. Bake 1 hour at 350°.

Marilyn Kay Herschberger

Angel Food Cake

1 pt. egg whites
1 tsp. vanilla
¼ tsp. almond flavoring
1½ tsp. cream of tartar
¼ tsp. salt

½ c. sugar
⅓ c. Jell-O, any flavor
1¼ c. flour
½ c. sugar

Beat first 5 ingredients until stiff. Beat in the ½ c. sugar and ⅓ c. Jell-O. Sift flour and second ½ c. sugar together, and fold into first mixture. Put in 10-inch tube pan. For plain white cake, omit the Jell-O and add ¾ c. sugar. Bake at 325° until done.

Mrs. Dan (Mary) Miller

Applesauce Spice Cupcakes

⅓ c. butter, softened
¾ c. sugar
2 eggs
1 tsp. vanilla extract
1⅓ c. flour
1 tsp. baking powder

½ tsp. baking soda
½ tsp. salt
1 tsp. ground cinnamon
½ tsp. ground nutmeg
⅛ tsp. ground cloves
¾ c. applesauce

Cream butter and sugar. Add eggs and vanilla; mix well. Combine dry ingredients; add to creamed mixture alternately with applesauce. Fill greased muffin cups to two-thirds full. Bake at 350° for 25 minutes. Frost with cream cheese frosting.

Naomi Engbretson

Chocolate Chip Cookies

6 sticks margarine
2 c. shortening
8 eggs
3 c. white sugar
3 c. brown sugar
8 tsp. vanilla

5 3-oz. pkgs. instant vanilla pudding
4 tsp. salt
4 tsp. baking soda
12 c. flour
2 12-oz. pkgs. chocolate chips

Mix well and bake at 350° for 8–10 minutes. Do not overbake.

Mrs. John (Carolyn) Otto

Chocolate Chip Cookies

3 c. vegetable oil
3 c. sugar
3 c. brown sugar
8 eggs
4 tsp. baking soda

4 tsp. salt
4 tsp. vanilla
4 tsp. water
10½ c. flour
3 c. chocolate chips

Mix vegetable oil and sugar. Add beaten eggs. Add flour, salt, and soda, which have been measured together. Add water and vanilla. Fold in chocolate chips. Drop by rounded teaspoonfuls onto cookie sheets. Bake at 350°. Makes approximately 12 dozen cookies.

Mrs. Ben (Anna Mary) Fisher

Chocolate Chip Cookies

1 pkg. yellow cake mix
2 eggs
½ c. vegetable oil
2 T. water

1 6-oz. pkg. chocolate chips
1 c. Rice Krispies
1 c. coconut

Mix all together and drop by teaspoonfuls onto cookie sheet. Bake until lightly browned; do not overbake. Very good.

Mrs. Edna Slabaugh

Do not expect God to use you as a
lighthouse somewhere
else if He can't use you as
a candle where you are.

Chocolate Chip Cookies

3 c. vegetable oil
2½ c. white sugar
2½ c. brown sugar
8 eggs
4 tsp. salt

4 tsp. baking soda
4 tsp. water
4 tsp. vanilla
10 c. flour
3 c. chocolate chips

Combine vegetable oil, white sugar, brown sugar, and eggs. Add salt, soda, water, vanilla, flour, and chocolate chips. Mix well. Drop on cookie sheet. Bake at 375° until barely done.

Mrs. Joe (Susie) Delagrange

Hershey's Chocolate Chip Cookies

1 c. butter or margarine
¾ c. packed brown sugar
¾ c. sugar
2 eggs
1 tsp. vanilla

2¼ c. flour
1 tsp. baking soda
½ tsp. salt
1 c. chopped nuts
2 c. chocolate chips

Drop onto ungreased cookie sheets. Bake at 375° for 8-10 minutes or until light brown. About 6 dozen cookies.

Deborah Slabaugh

Aunt Virgie's Peanut Butter Chocolate Cookies

1¼ c. butter or margarine, softened
2 c. white sugar
2 eggs
1 tsp. baking soda
½ tsp. salt

¾ c. cocoa
2 tsp. vanilla
2 c. flour
1 pkg. (1⅓ c.) large peanut butter chips

Mix ingredients in order given and stir well after each addition. Bake at 350° for 8 or 9 minutes or until set. Do not overbake, and cookies will be soft.

Mrs. Freeman (Wilma) Troyer

Peanut Butter Cookies

1½ c. margarine	4 tsp. vanilla
2 c. peanut butter	5 c. flour
2 c. white sugar	1 tsp. salt
2 c. brown sugar	3 tsp. baking soda
4 eggs, well-beaten	2 tsp. baking powder

Cream margarine and sugar; add eggs and peanut butter. Mix well. Add dry ingredients and vanilla. Form balls the size of a walnut and press out with a fork. Bake at 375° for 10-12 minutes.

Joanna Miller

Monster Cookies

6 eggs	2⅔ tsp. baking soda
⅓ lb. butter	9 c. oatmeal
1⅓ c. brown sugar	⅓ lb. chocolate chips
1⅓ c. white sugar	⅓ lb. M&M's
1½ T. plus 1 tsp. vanilla	⅓ lb. nuts (optional)
1½ lb. peanut butter	

Cream eggs and butter. Add brown sugar, white sugar, vanilla, and peanut butter. Mix well. Add soda and oatmeal. Next stir in chocolate chips, M&M's, and nuts. Bake at 350° for 10-15 minutes. (They burn very easily, so don't overbake.)

Mrs. Glen (Marilyn) Miller

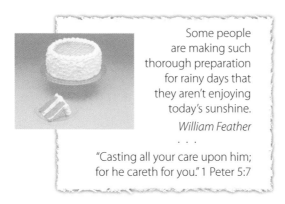

Some people are making such thorough preparation for rainy days that they aren't enjoying today's sunshine.

William Feather

. . .

"Casting all your care upon him; for he careth for you." 1 Peter 5:7

Everything Cookies

1 c. margarine	1 c. salad oil
1 c. brown sugar	2 tsp. vanilla
1 c. white sugar	3 c. flour
1 egg, beaten	1 tsp. salt
1 tsp. cream of tartar	1 tsp. baking soda
1 c. oatmeal	1 c. Rice Krispies
1 c. coconut	1 c. chocolate chips

Mix in order given. Drop by teaspoonful on ungreased cookie sheet. Bake at 350° for 10-15 minutes or until golden brown.

Emily Engbretson

Ranger Cookies

2 c. margarine or shortening	2 tsp. baking soda
2 c. sugar	1 tsp. salt
4 eggs	2 c. coconut
1 T. vanilla	2 c. chocolate chips
5 c. flour	8 c. Rice Krispies
2 tsp. baking powder	

Mix in order given. Bake at 400° until golden.

Irma Troyer

Lydia Cookies

1 c. shortening, margarine, or a combination	2 tsp. maple flavoring
1 c. white sugar	4 c. flour and about ¼ c. more
1 c. brown sugar	2 tsp. baking powder
2 eggs	2 tsp. baking soda
2 tsp. vanilla	½ c. hot water

Cream shortening and sugars. Add eggs and flavorings and blend well. Put soda in hot water and add to mixture, stirring well. Mix in flour with baking powder. Chill and roll out with a little flour. Cut into desired shapes. Bake at 350° until golden brown.

Mrs. Jerry (Ruth) Gingerich

Rocky Road Drop Cookies

Cookies:

1½ c. butter
1⅔ c. brown sugar
3 tsp. vanilla
3 beaten eggs
1½ c. semisweet chocolate
    morsels

4½ c. flour
1½ tsp. baking soda
1 c. milk
marshmallow halves (cut with scissors
    dipped in water)

Icing:

½ c. butter
½ c. milk

1 c. chocolate chips
½ tsp. vanilla
5 c. powdered sugar

Cream butter and brown sugar; stir in vanilla, eggs, milk, and chocolate. Add dry ingredients. Chill dough. Drop on a cookie sheet and bake at 450° for 8 minutes. Put marshmallow half on top of cookie (cut side down) and return to oven until marshmallow is soft (1 or 2 minutes).

For icing: Melt butter and chocolate chips. Stir in milk; add powdered sugar and vanilla; frost.

Mrs. Jerome (Rose) Graber

Double Crunchers Cookies

½ c. shortening
1 egg
½ c. brown sugar
½ tsp. vanilla
1 c. flour

½ tsp. baking soda
1 c. rolled oats
1 tsp. salt
1 c. coconut
1 c. cornflakes or Rice Krispies

Filling:

1 c. butterscotch chips
½ c. powdered sugar

1 T. water
½ c. cream cheese

Cream together shortening, sugar, egg, and vanilla. Add dry ingredients to make a stiff batter. Roll in balls and flatten on ungreased cookie sheet. Bake at 350° for 12 minutes. Makes 2 dozen. This also makes good bar cookies. For filling, melt chips in double boiler. Stir in remaining ingredients.

Mrs. John Almon (Elmina) Mast

Cornflake Cookies

6 c. cornflakes
1 c. peanut butter

1 c. corn syrup
1 c. sugar

Bring sugar and corn syrup to a boil. Add peanut butter. Pour over cornflakes. Stir until well mixed. Drop by tsp. on wax paper. Let cool. Serves 12.

Esther Delagrange

Brown Sugar Cookies

4 c. brown sugar
2 c. margarine or butter
8 c. flour, sifted
4 tsp. baking powder
1 T. vanilla

6 eggs, beaten
2 tsp. baking soda
¼ tsp. salt
1 c. milk

Cream butter and brown sugar together. Add eggs and vanilla and mix well. Add dry ingredients gradually along with milk. Bake at 350° for 10-15 minutes.

Ruby W. Mast

Brown Sugar Refrigerator Crisps

2 eggs, slightly beaten
2 c. brown sugar, packed
1 c. butter
3 tsp. vanilla

3½ c. unsifted flour
1 tsp. baking soda
½ tsp. salt
1 c. finely chopped walnuts, optional

Cream together eggs, sugar, butter, and vanilla. Combine flour, soda, and salt. Add to egg mixture. Blend well. Stir in nuts if used. Divide dough in half. Roll each half into a log, 2 inches in diameter, in waxed paper. Twist ends to shut. Refrigerate until firm, at least overnight. Cut into ¼-inch thick slices. Set slices 1 inch apart on ungreased cookie sheets. Bake at 350° for 10-12 minutes or until crisp. Makes 6 dozen cookies.

Mrs. Joe (Susie) Delagrange

The Authentic Amish Cookbook

Slice of Spice Cookies (Overnight)

6 c. flour
2 tsp. baking soda
2 tsp. cream of tartar
1 tsp. salt
1 c. butter

1 c. shortening
4 c. brown sugar, packed
4 eggs
2 tsp. vanilla
2 c. oatmeal

Mix first 4 ingredients and set aside. Cream butter, shortening, and sugar. Blend in eggs and vanilla. Stir in dry ingredients. Add oatmeal and mix well. Shape dough into rolls on waxed paper and chill overnight. When ready to bake, slice and dip each cookie in mixture of ¾ c. sugar and 6 tsp. cinnamon. Bake at 350°. (They are also good dipped in powdered sugar and cinnamon.)

Mrs. John (Carolyn) Otto

Raisin-Filled Cookies

Cookies:

1 c. shortening
2 c. sugar
2 eggs
5½ c. flour, approximately
1 tsp. salt

4 tsp. baking powder
1 tsp. baking soda
1 c. milk
2 tsp. vanilla

Filling:

2 c. raisins
1 c. sugar
2 c. water

2-4 T. Clear Jel
½ c. nuts
lemon juice

Cook filling and let cool. Roll out dough; cut in circles. Put 1 tsp. of filling on circle, then top with another one. (They don't need to be pressed together.) Bake at 350° until light in color.

Marjorie Mast

Do not condemn the judgment of another because it differs from your own. You may both be wrong.

Henry Wadsworth Longfellow

Cinnamon Lemon Cookies

1 c. sugar
½ c. butter
1 egg
1 tsp. vanilla
1½ c. flour
1½ tsp. ground cinnamon

1 tsp. baking powder
½ tsp. grated lemon peel
or extract
¼ tsp. salt
cinnamon sugar

Cream together sugar and butter. Beat in egg and vanilla. Combine flour, cinnamon, baking powder, lemon peel, and salt. Add to butter mixture. Blend well. Cover and refrigerate 2 hours or until firm. Shape dough into balls. Roll in cinnamon sugar. Set cookies on lightly greased cookie sheets. Bake at 350° for 10 minutes or until lightly browned. Makes 6 dozen cookies.

Esther Delagrange

Pineapple Cookies

1 c. shortening
1 c. brown sugar
1 c. white sugar
1 c. crushed pineapple
2 eggs, beaten
½ tsp. salt

1 tsp. baking soda
2 tsp. baking powder
4 c. flour
2 tsp. vanilla
1 c. chopped nuts, optional

Cream shortening and sugars; add eggs, pineapple, and flavoring. Sift flour; measure and sift with salt, soda, and baking powder. Add nuts. Bake on lightly greased sheet at 350° for 8-10 minutes. May be frosted with a frosting made of 3 c. powdered sugar, ¼ c. butter or margarine, and enough pineapple juice until it is the right consistency. Colored sprinkles on top are nice for holidays.

Beth Ann Yoder

Hershey's Kisses Cookies

1 can sweetened condensed milk
¾ c. peanut butter
Hershey's Kisses

1 tsp. vanilla
2 c. biscuit baking mix

Mix together milk and peanut butter. Add mix and vanilla. Stir well. Bake at 375° for 6-8 minutes. Do not overbake. Put kiss on top immediately after baking.

Mrs. Wilbur (Joann) Hochstetler

Pumpkin Cookies

1 c. shortening	1 tsp. baking powder
1 c. white sugar	1 tsp. baking soda
1 beaten egg	2 tsp. cinnamon
1 c. pumpkin	½ tsp. salt
2 tsp. vanilla	½ c. nuts
2 c. flour	½ c. dates

Topping (enough for 2 batches of cookies):

1 c. brown sugar	1 c. powdered sugar
3 T. butter	vanilla
4 T. milk	

Bake cookies at 375° for 10 minutes. For topping, mix the first 3 ingredients and boil for 2 minutes. Cool. Add 1 c. powdered sugar and vanilla.

Beth Ann Yoder

Bar Cookies

2 c. flour	1 tsp. salt
1 c. white sugar	1 tsp. baking powder
1 c. brown sugar	1 tsp. baking soda
1 c. vegetable oil	1 tsp. vanilla
2 c. quick oats	1 c. chocolate chips
3 eggs	

Bake at 350° for 20-30 minutes on a cookie sheet. Cut into bars when slightly cool.

Beth Ann Yoder

Chocolate Chip Bars

½ c. butter, melted	2 tsp. baking powder
2 c. sugar	1 tsp. vanilla
4 eggs (beat if you want a glossy top)	1½ tsp. salt
2 c. flour	2 c. chocolate chips

Mix together, then spread on cookie sheet. Bake at 350° for 25 minutes. Do not overbake.

Mrs. Norman (Marlena) Miller

Chocolate Chip Blondies

1½ c. packed brown sugar
½ c. butter, melted (no substitutes)
2 eggs, beaten
1 tsp. vanilla extract

1½ c. all-purpose flour
½ tsp. baking powder
½ tsp. salt
1 c. (6 oz.) semisweet chocolate chips

In a large bowl, combine brown sugar, butter, eggs, and vanilla just until blended. Combine flour, baking powder, and salt; add to brown sugar mixture. Stir in chocolate chips. Spread into a greased 9 x 13-inch baking pan. Bake at 350° for 18-20 minutes or until a toothpick inserted near the center comes out clean. Cool on a wire rack. Cut into bars. Makes 3 dozen.

Esther Delagrange

Brownies

2 c. sugar
4 T. water
⅔ c. butter
3 oz. chocolate chips

4 eggs, beaten
2 c. flour
½ tsp. salt
½ tsp. baking soda

Mix last 3 ingredients together and set aside. Mix first 3 ingredients in saucepan and bring to a boil. Add chocolate chips and stir. Cool. Add beaten eggs and stir well. Combine flour mixture with chocolate mixture. Blend well. Add nuts if desired. Bake at 325° for 30-35 minutes.

Mrs. Orlie (Mary) Troyer

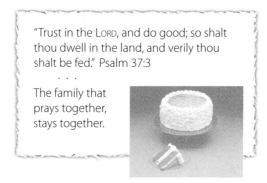

"Trust in the Lord, and do good; so shalt thou dwell in the land, and verily thou shalt be fed." Psalm 37:3

. . .

The family that prays together, stays together.

Fudge Brownies

2 c. sugar
1⅓ c. all-purpose flour
¾ c. baking cocoa
1 tsp. baking powder
½ tsp. salt

½ c. chopped nuts
⅔ c. vegetable oil
4 eggs, lightly beaten
2 tsp. vanilla

Combine sugar, flour, cocoa, baking powder, salt, and nuts. Set aside. Combine oil, eggs, and vanilla; add to dry ingredients. Do not overmix. Spread in 13 x 9-inch baking pan. Bake at 350° for 20-25 minutes. Yield: 2 dozen.

Mrs. Norman (Marlena) Miller

Fudge Bars

Oatmeal Mixture:
2 c. brown sugar
1 c. butter or margarine
2 eggs
2 tsp. vanilla
  Fudge Filling:
1 pkg. (12 oz.) chocolate chips
1 c. sweetened condensed milk
2 T. margarine

1 tsp. salt
1 tsp. baking soda
2½ c. flour
3 c. quick oats

½ tsp. salt
2 tsp. vanilla
1 c. nuts, chopped

Cream brown sugar, butter or margarine, eggs, and vanilla. Add salt, baking soda, flour, and oats and mix well. Spread ⅔ of mixture in 10 x 15-inch pan. Set the remainder aside. Combine filling ingredients in a double boiler and melt. Spread on top of oatmeal mixture. Top with the remainder of the oatmeal mixture. Bake at 350° for 20 minutes.

Priscilla Yoder

Be patient with the faults of others; they have to be patient with yours.

Molasses Bars

3 c. white sugar
1 lb. or 2 c. shortening
1 tsp. salt
1 pt. (2 c.) molasses or sorghum
5 eggs, beaten
3 T. baking soda

½ c. boiling water
5 c. wheat flour
5 c. white flour
2 lb. boiled raisins or
    chocolate chips (optional)

In a large bowl, mix sugar, salt, shortening, molasses, eggs, and soda. Add water and mix well; add flour and mix well. Add the goodies if you like. Take a handful and put on floured surface; form a roll 1-inch thick. Place on cookie sheets 2 inches apart and bake at 375° until lightly browned. Do not overbake. Cut in desired size. Delicious.

Mrs. Leroy (Viola) Mast

Fruit Bars

1¾ c. sugar
1 c. margarine
4 eggs
1 tsp. vanilla
3 c. flour

1½ tsp. baking powder
½ tsp. salt
1 qt. canned fruit pie filling or
    equivalent of thickened fresh
    berries or fruit

Cream sugar and margarine until fluffy. Add eggs and vanilla. Beat well. Sift dry ingredients and add to creamed mixture, stirring well until blended. Spread dough onto cookie sheet, reserving some of mixture for the top. Spread pie filling on top of dough, then drop remaining dough by teaspoons over filling. Bake at 350° for 35 minutes or until done. Spread on favorite vanilla frosting while still warm or drizzle all over with glaze. Serves 15.

Mrs. Reuben (Elizabeth) Luthy

Housework is something you do that no one notices until you don't do it.

Cherry Slices

1 c. margarine, melted
1¾ c. sugar
1 tsp. vanilla
2½ c. flour

1½ tsp. baking powder
4 eggs
1 can cherry pie filling

Combine margarine, sugar, flour, vanilla, baking powder, and eggs. Beat until fluffy. Spread half of dough on greased jelly-roll pan. Spread cherry pie filling over dough, then cover with remaining dough. Bake at 350° for 40 minutes. Cut into bars.

Mrs. Jerome (Rose) Graber

Lemon Cheese Bars

1 lemon cake mix
8 oz. cream cheese, softened
⅓ c. sugar

⅓ c. oil
1 T. lemon juice
2 eggs

Mix dry cake mix, 1 egg, and ⅓ c. oil until crumbly. Reserve 1 cup. Pat the rest of the mixture into an ungreased 9 x 13-inch pan. Bake 15 minutes at 350°. Beat cream cheese, sugar, lemon juice, and other egg until smooth. Spread over baked layer. Sprinkle the extra cup of crumbs on top and bake 15 more minutes. Cool and cut into squares. (Duncan Hines cake mix works best.)

Joanna Miller

Rhubarb Dream Bars

Crust:
1 c. butter
2 c. flour
Filling:
4 eggs
2 c. sugar
4 c. diced rhubarb

¾ c. powdered sugar

½ c. flour
½ tsp. salt

Mix crust and pat in bottom of 9 x 13-inch pan. Press down and bake 15 minutes at 350°. Mix filling together until smooth, adding rhubarb last. Spread over hot crust. Bake 45 minutes or until filling is lightly browned. Cool and cut in squares.

Mrs. James (Rosanna) Miller

Butterscotch Bars

½ c. butter
2 c. brown sugar
2 eggs
1 tsp. vanilla

2 c. flour
½ tsp. salt
2 tsp. baking powder

Melt butter and stir in sugar; add eggs and vanilla. Mix well. Next, add dry ingredients and mix. Spread batter evenly in a greased 10 x 15-inch pan. Bake for 30 minutes at 350°. Do not overbake.

Mrs. Wilmer (Clara Mae) Yoder

Wanda's Frosting

1 c. milk
2 T. cornstarch
pinch salt
1 stick butter

½ c. shortening
1 c. sugar
vanilla

Cook milk, cornstarch, and salt together. Cool, then add remaining ingredients and beat 4 minutes. This is a very fluffy, soft, and not-so-sweet frosting.

Lena Yoder

Quick Chocolate Glaze

⅔ c. sugar
3 T. milk

3 T. butter

Mix all ingredients and heat until boiling; boil 30 seconds. Stir in ½ c. chocolate chips until melted.

Mrs. Jonas (Elizabeth) Wagler

"He that is faithful in that which is least is faithful also in much." Luke 16:10

Icing for Red Velvet Cake

1 c. milk
¼ c. flour
¾ c. sugar

½ c. shortening
½ c. butter
1 tsp. vanilla

Combine milk and flour and cook until thick, stirring constantly with small wire whisk. Cool completely. Cream together remaining ingredients and beat into flour mixture. Beat until fluffy.

Mrs. Norman (Marlena) Miller

Frosting for Oatmeal Cake

6 T. margarine
1 c. brown sugar
¼ c. cream or rich milk

1½ c. coconut
1 tsp. vanilla

Heat margarine, brown sugar, and cream until bubbly. Then add coconut and vanilla. Spread over hot cake.

Mrs. Earl (Irma) Chupp

Notes

Soups and Vegetables

People of the Living God

Thy people shall be my people, and thy God my God. —Ruth 1:16

James Montgomery, 1771-1854

From *Harmonia Sacra*

1. Peo - ple of the liv - ing God, I have sought the world a - round;
2. Lone - ly I no lon - ger roam Like the cloud, the wind, the wave;
3. Tell me not of gain and loss, Ease, en - joy-ment, pomp, and pow'r;

Paths of sin and sor - row trod, Peace and com - fort no - where found:
Where you dwell shall be my home, Where you die shall be my grave;
Wel - come pov - er - ty and cross, Shame, re-proach, af - flic - tion's hour.

Now to you my spir - it turns,— Turns a fu - gi - tive un - blest;
Mine the God whom you a - dore; Your Re-deem - er shall be mine;
"Fol - low Me"— I know Thy voice; Je - sus, Lord, Thy steps I see;

Breth - ren, where your al - tar burns, Oh, re - ceive me in - to rest.
Earth can fill my soul no more,— Ev- ' ry i - dol I re - sign.
Now I take Thy yoke by choice, Light Thy bur - den now to me.

Cheeseburger Soup

½ lb. ground beef
¾ c. chopped onion
¾ c. shredded carrots
¾ c. diced celery
1 tsp. dried basil
1 tsp. dried parsley flakes
4 T. butter, divided
3 c. chicken broth

4 c. diced, peeled potatoes
¼ c. all-purpose flour
8 oz. processed American cheese,
  cubed (2 c.)
1½ c. milk
¾ tsp. salt
¼ to ½ tsp. pepper
¼ c. sour cream

Brown beef in 3-qt. saucepan; drain and set aside. In the same saucepan, sauté onion, carrots, celery, basil, and parsley in 1 T. butter until vegetables are tender, about 10 minutes. Add broth, potatoes, and beef; bring to a boil. Reduce heat; cover and simmer for 10-12 minutes or until potatoes are tender. Meanwhile, in a small skillet, melt remaining butter. Add flour; cook and stir for 3-5 minutes or until bubbly. Add to soup, bring to boil. Cook and stir for 2 minutes. Reduce heat to low. Add cheese, milk, salt, and pepper; cook and stir until cheese melts. Remove from heat; blend in sour cream. Serves 8.

Amy Elizabeth Kauffman

Chili Soup

2½ lb. fried hamburger
1 rounded T. chili powder
½ tsp. red pepper
½ c. chopped onion
3 tsp. salt

1 c. Perma-flo
1 qt. catsup
2 28-oz. cans pork and beans
3 qt. water
1 c. brown sugar

In an 8-qt. kettle, mix chili powder, pepper, salt, Perma-flo, catsup, brown sugar, and water. Bring to a boil and cook 1 minute. Add hamburger, pork and beans, and onions. Simmer on low heat, stirring often. Or may put in roaster and bake in oven at 325° for 1 hour.

Mrs. Omer (Martha) Miller

Christ does not leave the soul when extraordinary joys and comforts leave it.

Spicy Chili

1 lb. ground beef	1 qt. diced tomatoes or tomato juice
1 medium onion, chopped	1 can kidney beans
5 tsp. seasoning mix	

Spicy Chili Seasoning Mix:

½ c. chili powder	1 T. garlic powder
5 tsp. ground coriander	2 tsp. dried oregano
5 tsp. ground cumin	1 tsp. cayenne pepper

Fry ground beef in oil with onion. Add 2 tsp. seasoning mix. Heat tomatoes and beans; add meat mixture and 3 more tsp. seasoning mix. Simmer 10 minutes. Serves 6.

Mrs. Elvie (Rebekah) Miller

Taco Soup

2 lb. hamburger, browned with onion, salt, and pepper	1 qt. pizza sauce
	1 qt. water
1 pkg. taco seasoning	1 can hot chili beans

Combine all ingredients, heat, and serve with sour cream, grated cheddar cheese, and crumbled taco chips.

Mrs. David (Rhoda) Miller

Turkey Chowder

3 c. chicken broth	3 c. chopped, cooked turkey
4 medium diced, cooked potatoes	4 cloves garlic, minced (optional)
4 strips bacon, fried and crumbled	3 T. butter
1 large onion, diced and sautéed	4½ c. light cream

Mix ingredients in 3-qt. kettle and heat. Do not boil. Serves 10.

Mrs. Jonas (Elizabeth) Wagler

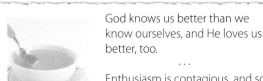

God knows us better than we know ourselves, and He loves us better, too.

. . .

Enthusiasm is contagious, and so is the lack of it.

Cheesy Turkey Chowder

2 frozen turkey wings or 1 drumstick
1 tsp. salt
1 medium onion, chopped
1 c. carrots, chopped
1 c. celery, chopped
1 c. potatoes, diced
1 c. shredded cheese
2 c. milk
6 T. flour
¼ c. butter

Place frozen turkey wings in a large saucepan. Add water until meat is covered. Add salt and onion. Bring to a boil. Reduce heat and simmer until meat is tender. Remove from broth; debone meat and cut in small pieces. To 4 cups broth (add water to make 4 cups if necessary), add carrots, celery, and potatoes. Simmer until tender. Gradually blend milk into flour until smooth. Stir in broth along with butter and cheese. Cook over medium heat until thickened, stirring constantly. Add turkey meat.

Mrs. Orlie (Mary) Troyer

Baked Potato Soup

⅔ c. margarine
⅔ c. flour*
7 c. milk
4 large potatoes, baked and chopped
¼ c. onion, chopped (optional)
12 bacon strips, cooked and crumbled
1¼ c. shredded cheddar cheese
1 c. sour cream
¾ tsp. salt
½ tsp. black pepper
   *(I use more like a heaping ⅓ cup; otherwise it gets too thick.)

In large soup kettle, melt margarine; stir in flour. Heat and stir until smooth. Add milk, stirring constantly until thickened. Add potatoes and onions. Bring to a boil, stirring constantly. Reduce heat, simmer 10 minutes. Add remaining ingredients. Stir until cheese is melted. Serves 10.

Regina Miller

The beauty of life is to be found in thoughts that rise above the needs of self.

. . .

Help me to look on others, O Lord, with love and a desire to help, rather than with envy.

Country Potato Soup

3 c. diced potatoes
½ c. carrots
½ c. onions
1½ c. water
2 tsp. chicken soup base
2 c. milk

1 c. sour cream
2 T. flour
1 tsp. chives
½ tsp. salt
Velveeta cheese

Put first 5 ingredients in pan; cover and cook about 20 minutes. Add 1 c. milk; heat. Mix sour cream, flour, chives, salt, and other c. milk. Stir into soup; cook until thickened. Add a few slices Velveeta cheese and stir until melted.

Beth Ann Yoder

Chicken Corn Chowder

1 pt. chicken bits
1 pt. chicken broth
1 can corn
1 can cream of mushroom soup

1 can cream of chicken soup
2 soup cans water
¾ c. minute rice
1 medium onion

Place chicken bits and broth in 4-qt. kettle. Cook until hot; add remaining ingredients and cook until rice is soft. Season to taste with chicken base, salt, and pepper.

Mrs. Wilbur (Joann) Hochstetler

Cheese Soup

1 c. carrots
1 c. celery
1 c. onions
3 c. potatoes
2 cans cream of chicken soup

1 pkg. frozen California Blend
    vegetables or mixed vegetables
1 c. water
1 lb. Velveeta cheese

Dice carrots, celery, onions, and potatoes. Cook in 1 qt. of water for 20 minutes or until tender. Add remaining ingredients. Cook slowly on low heat. Burns easily. Four chicken bouillon cubes may be added. Salt to taste.

Mrs. Wilmer (Clara Mae) Yoder
Mrs. Perry (Delores) Herschberger

Chilly Day Stew

1 large carrot	2 T. macaroni
4 onions	1 tsp. salt
1 qt. potatoes, peeled and diced	water enough to cover
2 T. rice	1 pt. cream

Add ingredients in order given, except cream, to a large kettle of boiling water. Cook slowly until tender. When ready to serve, add cream. Mix well, but do not boil again. Serve with croutons, crackers, or hot toast. Note: You can substitute milk and butter for the cream.

Mrs. Nathan (Mattie) Miller

Big Valley Bean Soup

½ c. cooked navy beans	3 c. bread cubes, approximately
2 T. butter	salt and pepper to taste
3 to 4 c. milk	

Melt butter; add beans and simmer for 5 minutes. Add milk and heat to boiling point. Add bread cubes (it's best to use bread that's several days old). Use more or less bread for desired thickness. Serve with pickles and fresh apple pie!

Mrs. Stephen (Amelia) Miller

Lentil Soup

¼ c. olive oil	1 qt. broth, or
2 c. lentils	1 qt. water and beef bouillon
1 carrot, grated	salt to taste
½ onion, chopped	1 T. basil
1 tsp. minced garlic	¼ tsp. pepper
½ to 1 pt. tomato juice	

Saute lentils, carrot, onion, and garlic in olive oil for 5 minutes. Add broth, tomato juice, and seasonings. Cook until lentils are tender, adding water as needed. Serves 5-6.

Mrs. Reuben (Elizabeth) Luthy

Summer Corn Roast

2 ears of sweet corn per person with husks on

Pick early in the morning. In large washtub, sink corn in cold water, weighing it down to be sure it's all the way under water. Soak all day. Shortly before serving time, drain the corn. Roast it in your barbecue grill or over charcoal, leaving the husks in place. When done, place in a brown paper bag and fold down top to keep hot until you're ready to eat. Serve with butter and salt.

Mrs. Orlie (Mary) Troyer

A Garden for Mothers

Plant 3 rows of squash:
1. squash gossip
2. squash criticism
3. squash indifference

Plant 7 rows of peas:
1. prayer
2. promptness
3. perseverance
4. politeness
5. preparedness
6. purity
7. patience

Plant 7 rows of lettuce:
1. let us be unselfish and loyal
2. let us be faithful to duty
3. let us search the Scriptures
4. let us not be weary in well-doing
5. let us be obedient in all things
6. let us be truthful
7. let us love one another

No garden is complete without turnips:
1. turn up with a smile—even when things are difficult
2. turn up with determination to do your best in God's service

After planting, may you grow in grace and in the knowledge of our Lord and Savior, Jesus Christ (2 Peter 3:18). May you reap rich results!

Meats and Main Dishes

The Lily of the Valley

I am the rose of Sharon, and the lily of the valleys. —Song of Solomon 2:1

Charles W. Fry, 1837-1882   Arr. from William S. Hays, 1837-1907

1. I have found a friend in Je-sus, He's ev-'ry-thing to me, He's the
2. O He all my griefs has tak-en, and all my sor-rows borne; In temp-
3. He will nev-er, nev-er leave me, nor yet for-sake me here, While I

fair-est of ten thousand to my soul; The Lil-y of the Val-ley, in
ta-tion He's my strong and mighty tow'r; I have all for Him for-sak-en, and
live by faith and do His bless-ed will; A wall of fire a-bout me, I've

D. S. Lil-y of the Val-ley, the
FINE

Him a-lone I see All I need to cleanse and make me ful-ly whole.
all my i-dols torn From my heart, and now He keeps me by His pow'r.
noth-ing now to fear, With His man-na He my hun-gry soul shall fill,

bright and morn-ing star, He's the fair-est of ten thou-sand to my soul.

In sor-row He's my com-fort, in trou-ble He's my stay,
Tho' all the world for-sake me, and Sa-'tan tempt me sore,
Then sweep-ing up to glo-ry to see His bless-ed face,

D. S.

He tells me ev-'ry care on Him to roll, He's the
Thro' Je-sus I shall safe-ly reach the goal, He's the
Where riv-ers of de-light shall ev-er roll, He's the

Scrambled Egg Casserole

2 T. butter
2½ T. flour
2 c. milk
½ tsp. salt
⅛ tsp. ground pepper
1 c. American cheese, shredded
   Topping:
¼ c. melted butter

1 c. cubed ham
¼ c. chopped green onion
3 T. melted butter
1 dozen eggs, beaten
1 4-oz. can mushrooms,
   sliced and drained

2¼ c. soft bread crumbs

To make cheese sauce, melt butter; blend in flour and cook for 1 minute. Gradually stir in milk; cook until thick. Add salt, pepper, and cheese; stir until cheese melts. Set aside. Saute ham and green onion in 3 T. butter until onion is tender. Add eggs and cook until eggs are set; stir in the mushrooms and cheese sauce. Spoon eggs into greased 9 x 13-inch pan. Combine topping ingredients; spread over top. Cover; chill overnight. Uncover and bake at 350° for 30 minutes.

Naomi Engbretson

Baked Omelet Roll

6 eggs, beaten
1 c. milk
½ c. flour
½ tsp. salt

¼ tsp. pepper
1 c. shredded cheddar cheese
½ c. diced cooked ham
1 c. fried potatoes

Beat first 5 ingredients together. Pour into a greased 13 x 9 x 2-inch baking pan. Bake at 450° for 18-20 minutes or until eggs are set. Sprinkle potatoes, ham, and cheese over top. Roll up omelet in pan. Place seam-side down on serving platter. Cut into 6 slices. Serve with maple syrup.

Mrs. Omer (Martha) Miller

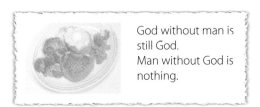

God without man is
still God.
Man without God is
nothing.

Brunch Casserole

½ lb. bacon, fried and crumbled
½ c. onion
12 eggs
1 c. milk
1 c. shredded cheddar cheese

1 16-oz. pkg. frozen hash brown
  potatoes, thawed
1 tsp. salt
½ tsp. pepper
¼ tsp. dill weed

In the bacon drippings, saute onion until tender; remove with slotted spoon. Beat eggs and milk in large bowl. Stir in hash browns, cheese, salt, pepper, dill, onion, and bacon. Pour into 9 x 13-inch baking dish. Bake uncovered at 350° for 35-45 minutes or until a knife inserted near center comes out clean. Serves 6-8.

Mrs. Omer (Martha) Miller

Egg Casserole

8 slices bread, cubed
2 c. cheese, grated
4 to 6 eggs
2½ c. milk
1 can mushrooms

1 10¾-oz. can mushroom soup
1 lb. sausage, ham, or bacon
¾ tsp. dry mustard
½ tsp. garlic powder

Fry meat and drain. Grease 9 x 13-inch pan. Put bread, meat, and cheese in pan. Mix rest of ingredients together and pour over. Let stand overnight. Bake at 300° for 1½ hours.

Mrs. Ernest (Sara) Schrock

Stove-Top Casserole

peeled shredded potatoes
ground beef
diced onion

Velveeta cheese
salt
pepper

Put in layers in well-greased skillet: potatoes, beef, onion, one layer each. Season to taste; cover and put on low heat on top of stove. Do not stir. Cooking time will vary depending on amount of casserole. A full skillet takes 45-60 minutes. Top with cheese when done. Delicious and simple! For large amounts, layer these same ingredients twice each in a roaster and bake in oven.

Mrs. Marcus (Mary) Gingerich

The Authentic Amish Cookbook

Farmhouse Barbecue Muffins

1 10-oz. tube refrigerated
  buttermilk biscuits
1 lb. ground beef
½ c. ketchup

3 T. brown sugar
1 T. cider vinegar
½ tsp. chili powder
1 c. (4-oz.) shredded cheese

Separate dough into 10 biscuits; flatten into 5-inch circles. Press each into the bottom and up the sides of a greased muffin cup and set aside. Brown ground beef in skillet and drain. Mix ketchup, brown sugar, vinegar, and chili powder in small bowl; stir until smooth. Add to meat and mix well. Divide the meat mixture among biscuit-lined muffin cups, using about ¼ c. for each. Sprinkle with cheese. Bake at 375° for 18-20 minutes or until golden brown. Cool 5 minutes before removing from tin and serving. Serves 10.

Mrs. Jerome (Rose) Graber

Jiffy Chicken Muffin Supper

1 medium onion
2 c. potatoes
2 c. carrots
1 c. celery
1 c. peas
2 c. chicken
  Muffins:
1½ c. flour (we use half wheat)
1 T. sugar
2 tsp. baking powder
½ tsp. salt

2 c. broth
1 tsp. salt
2 tsp. chicken base
¼ tsp. pepper
water to cover
may add parsley if you like

1 egg
½ c. milk
2 T. melted shortening

Boil together vegetables until soft; add the rest and thicken with milk and flour through shaker. Keep prepared chicken warm while preparing muffins. Mix muffin ingredients well; drop by rounded tablespoon onto creamed chicken. Bake at 425° for 30 minutes or until muffins are golden.

Mrs. Leroy (Viola) Mast

"A talebearer revealeth secrets: but he that is of a faithful spirit concealeth the matter." Proverbs 11:13

Chicken Gumbo

9 slices of bread
4 c. cooked chicken
4 eggs, beaten
1 c. chicken broth
1 c. milk

1 tsp. salt
9 slices Velveeta cheese
1 can cream of celery soup
1 can cream of mushroom soup

Put cubed bread in bottom of buttered casserole dish. Put chicken on top of bread. Mix eggs, broth, milk, and salt. Pour over bread and chicken. Put cheese slices on this, then soup on cheese. Top with buttered bread crumbs. Bake uncovered for 1 hour at 350°.

Mrs. Wilmer (Clara Mae) Yoder

Huntington Chicken

1 hen, cooked and deboned
4 c. chicken broth
   Thickening for broth:
8 T. flour
¾ to 1 c. milk

2 c. macaroni, cooked and drained
1 c. cheese

1 T. chicken seasoning
salt to taste

Melt the cheese into the thickened broth. Pour over macaroni and chicken meat. Do not overstir or meat will get stringy. Pour into casserole dish and top with buttered bread crumbs. Bake at 350° for ½ hour. Serves 10.

Mrs. Norman (Marlena) Miller

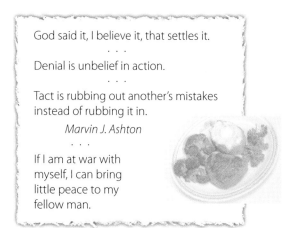

God said it, I believe it, that settles it.

· · ·

Denial is unbelief in action.

· · ·

Tact is rubbing out another's mistakes instead of rubbing it in.
    Marvin J. Ashton

· · ·

If I am at war with myself, I can bring little peace to my fellow man.

Huntington Chicken

1 qt. boneless chicken pieces	½ lb. Velveeta cheese, chopped
1 qt. chicken broth, flavored with	⅓ c. flour
1 to 2 T. chicken soup base	1 c. cream
2 c. noodles	1 egg yolk
4 to 6 hard-boiled eggs, finely chopped	salt and pepper to taste
(optional)	

Heat broth and chicken until boiling. Mix flour, cream, and egg yolk together and stir into broth until thickened. Boil noodles in salted water; drain. Mix all ingredients together and pour into a 3- to 4-qt. casserole dish. Top with potato chips or toasted bread crumbs and bake for 20-30 minutes at 350°. Variation: ¾ c. cheese powder may be added to broth instead of using Velveeta cheese. Serves 10.

Mrs. Noah (Fannie) Yoder

Baked Chicken

2½ to 3 lb. chicken	3 c. finely crushed Ritz crackers
Italian dressing	

Layer pieces of chicken in pan; pour Italian dressing over each piece. Marinate for 24 hours. Remove chicken from sauce; discard juice. Roll each piece of chicken in cracker crumbs. Place on cookie sheet. Bake at 350° for 1 hour.

Mrs. Omer (Martha) Miller

Crispy Baked Chicken

½ c. cornmeal	¼ tsp. pepper
½ c. flour	1 3 to 3½-lb. frying chicken, cut up
1½ tsp. salt	½ c. milk
1½ tsp. chili powder	⅓ c. butter or margarine, melted
½ tsp. dried oregano	

Combine the first 6 ingredients. Dip chicken in milk, then roll in the cornmeal mixture. Place in a greased 13 x 9-inch baking pan. Drizzle with butter. Bake uncovered at 375° for 50-55 minutes or until juices run clear.

Mrs. Norman (Marlena) Miller
Mrs. Monroe (Elsie) Miller

Honey-Mustard Baked Chicken

2 whole chickens, cut up	¼ c. Dijon mustard
½ c. butter or margarine	1 tsp. curry powder
½ c. honey	½ tsp. salt

Place chicken in large shallow baking pan. In saucepan, melt butter; stir in remaining ingredients and heat through. Brush glaze over chicken. Bake at 350° for 1¼ hours or until chicken is golden brown. Baste chicken frequently with sauce while baking. Serves 6-8.

Beth Ann Yoder

Venison Patties

3 lb. venison	1 tsp. onion salt
4 eggs	1½ tsp. salt
1½ c. milk	1½ tsp. pepper
1 tsp. garlic salt	2 c. cracker crumbs

Mix well and fry.

Mrs. Joe (Susie) Delagrange

Corned Beef

50 lb. beef (roasts, steaks, or any choice cuts)
2 scant qt. salt
  Brine:

¼ lb. baking soda	2 T. liquid smoke
¼ lb. saltpeter	water enough to cover meat well
2 lb. brown sugar	

Layer meat with salt in a large crock or similar suitable container. Let stand overnight. Then rinse off lightly and pack in crock again. Make brine. Place meat in brine. It will be cured and ready for use in 2 weeks. It can then be cut in suitable pieces and canned (cold pack 3 hours) or put in freezer. If crock is kept in a cold place, meat may be kept in brine and used anytime within 3 months. Flavor is improved when kept over 6 weeks. Tastes like ham.

Mrs. Leroy (Viola) Mast

Western Roast Beef

1 large beef roast	1 large onion

Sauce:

1 c. water	1 c. catsup
1½ tsp. salt	¼ tsp. Tabasco sauce
¼ tsp. chili powder	½ tsp. mustard
1 T. brown sugar	

Slice raw beef roast about ½-inch thick and layer with onion slices in pan that has a tightly fitting cover. Splash a little sauce on each layer and be sure the sauce reaches to cover the top layer. Bake at 350° for 3 hours or more until beef starts to fall apart. For a large crowd, prepare a 6-qt. cooker full and bake all day at 225°. Take the cover off for the last ½ hour to reduce moisture.

Mrs. Orlie (Mary) Troyer

Meat Loaf

1½ lb. hamburger	1 tsp. salt
¾ c. quick rolled oats	¼ tsp. pepper
¼ c. chopped onions	¾ c. milk
1 egg, beaten	½ c. pizza sauce

Sauce:

⅓ c. ketchup	1 T. mustard
2 T. brown sugar	

Mix meat loaf ingredients well. Pack firmly in baking dish. Mix the sauce and pour over meat loaf. Bake 1¼ hour at 350°.

Mrs. John (Carolyn) Otto

No door is too difficult for the key of love to open.

Meat Loaf

1½ lb. ground beef	2 tsp. salt
¾ c. oatmeal	¼ tsp. pepper
2 eggs, beaten	1 c. tomato juice
¼ c. chopped onion	

Sauce:

½ c. ketchup	2 T. brown sugar
1 T. mustard	

Combine ingredients thoroughly and pack firmly into loaf pan or 9 x 9-inch pan. Top with sauce. Bake at 350° for 1 hour. Let stand 5 minutes before slicing.

Mrs. Loyal (Dorcas) Gingerich

Meat Loaf

4 lb. ground beef	3 c. crushed crackers
4 eggs	2 c. ketchup
2 tsp. seasoned salt	1 tsp. black pepper
1 c. chopped onion	2 tsp. salt

Sauce:

1 c. ketchup	½ c. brown sugar
2 T. mustard	

Beat eggs and add remaining ingredients. Press firmly into 9 x 13-inch pan. Mix sauce; pour on top of meat loaf. Bake at 350° for 1 hour, covered.

Mrs. Joe (Susie) Delagrange
Irma Troyer

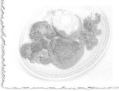

When you sneer and point your finger of scorn, three fingers are pointing back at you.

Pizza Meat Loaf

2 lb. ground beef
1 c. cracker crumbs
½ c. grated Parmesan cheese
2 tsp. pepper
1 c. (4 oz.) shredded mozzarella
  cheese

1 c. milk
½ c. chopped onion
2 eggs
1 tsp. oregano leaves
1 8-oz. can pizza sauce

Combine meat, crumbs, milk, onion, Parmesan cheese, eggs, and seasoning. Mix lightly. Press meat mixture into an 8-inch pan. Bake at 350° for 45 minutes. Pour off drippings. Spread pizza sauce over meat. Bake 10 minutes longer. Sprinkle with cheese. Return to oven until cheese begins to melt. Garnish with peppers, if desired.

Mrs. Glen (Marilyn) Miller

Barbecued Meatballs

Meatballs:
3 lb. hamburger
12 oz. milk
1 c. oatmeal
1 c. cracker crumbs
2 eggs
  Sauce:
2 c. catsup
1 c. brown sugar
½ tsp. liquid smoke

½ c. chopped onion
½ tsp. garlic powder
2 tsp. salt
½ tsp. pepper
2 tsp. chili powder

½ tsp. garlic powder
¼ c. chopped onion, optional

Combine meatball ingredients (mixture will be soft) and shape into walnut-size balls. Place in 9 x 13-inch pan. Combine sauce ingredients and stir until sugar is dissolved. Pour over meatballs. Bake at 350° for 50-60 minutes.

Mrs. Perry (Delores) Herschberger
Mrs. Jerry (Ruth) Gingerich

Yesterday is gone.
Tomorrow may never come.
Today is a gift....
That's why it's called "the Present."

Barbecued Meatballs

3 lb. ground beef
1¾ c. milk
2 c. quick oats
2 eggs
1 c. chopped onions
½ tsp. pepper
2 tsp. chili powder

½ tsp. garlic powder
2 tsp. salt
2 c. ketchup
1½ c. brown sugar
2 T. liquid smoke
½ tsp. garlic powder
½ c. minced onion

Mix first 9 ingredients together and shape into balls. Place in 9 x 13-inch baking pan. Mix and heat last 5 ingredients until dissolved and pour over meatballs. Cover pan with foil. Bake at 350° for 1 hour.

Mrs. Wilmer (Clara Mae) Yoder

Poor Man's Steak

3 lb. hamburger
1 c. cracker crumbs
1 c. milk

1½ tsp. salt
½ tsp. pepper
1 c. mushroom soup

Mix hamburger, cracker crumbs, milk, salt, and pepper together. Press into a cookie sheet and put into refrigerator overnight. In the morning cut into pieces, 3 or 4 inches square, and roll in flour. Brown in frying pan. Lay in roaster and pour undiluted soup over meat. Bake in 350° oven for 1 hour. Serves 6-8.

Mrs. Norman (Marlena) Miller

Pizza Pasta Casserole

2 lb. ground beef
1 large onion
2 jars (28 oz. each) spaghetti sauce
8 oz. sliced pepperoni

1 16-oz. pkg. spiral pasta,
  cooked and drained
4 c. (16 oz.) shredded mozzarella
  cheese

Cook beef and onion until meat is no longer pink; drain. Stir in spaghetti sauce and pasta. Transfer to two greased 9 x 13-inch baking dishes. Sprinkle with cheese. Arrange pepperoni over top. Cover and freeze 1 casserole for up to 3 months. Bake the second one uncovered at 350° for 25-30 minutes or until heated through. To use frozen casserole, thaw in refrigerator overnight. Bake at 350° for 35-40 minutes or until heated through. Each casserole serves 8-10.

Mrs. Nathan (Mattie) Miller

Pizza Rice Casserole

1½ c. raw rice
3 c. water
2 eggs
1 tsp. oregano
¼ c. Parmesan cheese
¼ tsp. garlic powder
1½ to 2 lb. ground beef

1 pt. pizza sauce
pepperoni
mushrooms
olives
onions
mozzarella cheese

Sprinkle rice evenly in greased 9 x 13-inch pan. Mix eggs, oregano, Parmesan cheese, garlic powder, and water and pour over rice. Fry ground beef; season as you do pizza. Add pizza sauce. Spread over rice mixture. Sprinkle over top: pepperoni, mushrooms, olives, and onions. Bake at 350° for 1¼ hours. Remove from oven and sprinkle liberally with mozzarella cheese. Return to oven until cheese melts.

Beth Ann Yoder

Pizza Casserole

2½ lb. hamburger
1 onion, finely chopped
½ c. spaghetti noodles
1 qt. pizza sauce
1 c. sour cream
3½ T. Miracle Whip dressing
3 c. grated cheese

1 7-oz. (small) can mushroom pieces
1⅓ c. flour
2 tsp. baking powder
⅔ tsp. salt
½ c. milk
¼ c. cooking oil

Fry hamburger with onion. Cook spaghetti. Mix flour, baking powder, and salt together. Add milk and oil all at once. Mix well. Press into 9 x 13-inch baking pan. Put hamburger on top of crust; spread pizza sauce over hamburger, then spoon spaghetti and mushrooms over sauce. Mix together sour cream, Miracle Whip dressing, and cheese (I also add 1-2 T. sour cream and onion powder) and pour over top. Bake at 350°.

Anna Yoder

One way to do great things for Christ is to do little things for others.

Mom's Lasagna

spaghetti sauce; either meat
or plain is good
1 16-oz. container cottage cheese
2 eggs

1 c. Parmesan cheese
1 16-oz. box lasagna noodles,
uncooked
mozzarella cheese, shredded

Mix cottage cheese, eggs, and Parmesan cheese; set aside. In 9 x 13-inch cake pan, spread a layer of spaghetti sauce, layer of uncooked noodles, layer of spaghetti sauce, and then a layer of cheese sauce. Repeat process until pan is full, ending with spaghetti sauce. Sprinkle a layer of mozzarella over all. (You may also layer mozzarella throughout if you wish.) Bake at 350° for 45 minutes to 1 hour or until noodles are done. Serves 9.

Mrs. Reuben (Elizabeth) Luthy

No-Fuss Lasagna

1½ lb. hamburger, fried and
seasoned with salt
2 tsp. oregano
¾ tsp. garlic powder, optional
3 c. pizza sauce
2½ c. water

12 uncooked lasagna noodles
4 oz. cream cheese
¼ c. milk
½ c. onion, chopped fine
1 c. mozzarella cheese

Add oregano and garlic powder to hamburger; stir in 2½ c. pizza sauce. Layer noodles and meat mixture alternately in cake pan, beginning and ending with 4 noodles. Put water over all, then spread with ½ c. pizza sauce. Cover thickly with foil and bake at 350° for 1½ hours or until the noodles are tender. Mix cream cheese, milk, and onion and spread over top. Sprinkle cheese on top and return to oven until cheese is melted. One can refried or mild chili beans may be added to the hamburger mixture and 1 c. sour cream substituted for cream cheese and milk.

Mrs. Norman (Marlena) Miller

A suffering Christian
is one whom God has
under special treatment.

Quick Turkey Nachos

1 lb. ground turkey or ground beef	½ c. salsa
1 pkg. (1¼ oz.) taco seasoning mix	½ c. shredded cheddar cheese
¾ c. water	½ c. Monterey Jack cheese
tortilla chips	chopped lettuce, tomatoes,
½ c. sour cream	and/or green onions

Brown meat in skillet. Add taco seasoning and water; simmer for 15 minutes. Put tortilla chips on plate, layer with meat mixture, sour cream, salsa, cheese, and vegetables. Variation: I use whatever cheeses I have on hand.

Mrs. Wilbur (Joann) Hochstetler

Burrito Casserole

2 cans cream of mushroom soup	refried beans, if desired
16 oz. sour cream	soft burrito shells
3 lb. hamburger, browned	cheese, lettuce, tomatoes
2 pkg. taco seasoning mix	

Mix soups with sour cream. Mix hamburger with taco seasonings. Mix refried beans with hamburger if you want to. Cover with burrito shells. Bake at 350° for 45 minutes to 1 hour. Layer cheese over top when done baking. When ready to serve, top with lettuce and tomatoes. This makes a big roaster half full.

Mrs. James (Rosanna) Miller

Wet Burritos

flour or corn tortillas	1 can cream of mushroom soup
1 lb. hamburger	1 can refried beans
1 pkg. taco seasoning	cheddar cheese, shredded
16 oz. sour cream	

Prepare hamburger with taco seasoning as directed on package. Add refried beans to hamburger. Mix soup and sour cream together and spread half on bottom of baking dish. Fill tortillas with meat mixture and place in baking dish. Spread remaining soup and sour cream mixture on top. Top with cheddar cheese. Bake at 325° for 30 to 40 minutes.

Mrs. Steve (Edith) Engbretson

Taco Bake

2 c. Bisquick*
½ c. water
1 lb. ground beef
1 can refried beans, optional
½ pkg. taco seasoning

2 tomatoes, chopped
1 green pepper, diced
1 c. sour cream
⅔ c. Miracle Whip dressing
1 c. Colby cheese

Mix Bisquick (*using a biscuit recipe works fine too) and water; put in bottom of a 9 x 13-inch pan. Brown hamburger with onions, then mix in beans and taco seasoning. Place on top of batter. Sprinkle diced vegetables on top. Mix sour cream, dressing, and cheese; spread on top. Sprinkle with additional cheese. Bake 30 minutes at 350°. Delicious! Serves 10.

Regina Miller

Easy Taco Skillet Meal

1 lb. ground beef
1 pt. tomato juice
1 c. uncooked rice
1 c. shredded cheddar cheese
¾ c. water
2 T. brown sugar

1 pkg. taco seasoning
shredded lettuce
chopped onions
sour cream
salsa or picante sauce

Brown ground beef in a large skillet with a lid. Add tomato juice, water, brown sugar, seasonings, and rice. Simmer for 20 minutes or until rice is tender, stirring several times. Top with cheese and let melt. Serve with shredded lettuce, onions, sour cream, and salsa. Serves 8.

Rita Miller

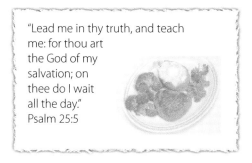

"Lead me in thy truth, and teach me: for thou art the God of my salvation; on thee do I wait all the day."
Psalm 25:5

Taco Quiche

2 lb. ground beef
2 1.25-oz. pkg. taco seasoning
4 eggs
¾ c. milk
1¼ c. biscuit/baking mix
dash pepper

½ c. sour cream
2 to 3 c. lettuce, chopped
¾ c. chopped tomato
¼ c. chopped green pepper
¼ c. chopped green onions
2 c. shredded cheese

Brown beef in skillet; drain. Add taco seasoning and prepare according to package directions. Spoon meat into greased 9 x 13-inch baking dish. In a bowl, beat eggs and milk. Add biscuit mix and pepper; mix well. Pour over meat. Bake uncovered at 400° for 20-25 minutes. Cool 5-10 minutes. Spread sour cream over top; sprinkle with lettuce, tomatoes, green pepper, onions, and cheese. Serve immediately. Serves 8.

Mrs. Jerome (Rose) Graber

Enchiladas

1½ lb. browned hamburger
1 pt. pizza sauce
1 10½-oz. can cream of chicken soup

8 to 10 soft tortillas
1 c. shredded cheese

Add 1 c. pizza sauce and soup to browned hamburger; simmer. Divide mixture on tortillas. Roll up and put in greased cake pan. Pour remaining pizza sauce over top and cover with cheese. Bake at 350° for 20 minutes. Serve with lettuce and sour cream.

Mrs. Omer (Martha) Miller

Enchilada Casserole

12 corn tortillas
2 lb. hamburger
2 T. chili powder
½ tsp. garlic powder
1 medium onion, chopped

1 15-oz. can tomato sauce
salt and pepper
1 c. grated Colby or cheddar cheese
1 10½-oz. can cream of chicken soup
¾ c. milk

Brown meat, garlic, and onion. Add tomato sauce, chili powder, salt, and pepper. Heat 9 x 13-inch pan. Line bottom with 6 tortillas. Add meat mixture on top. Cover with 6 more tortillas. Spread chicken soup over these, then milk. Cover with cheese. Bake 25 minutes at 350°. Serves 12-14.

Mrs. Jonas (Elizabeth) Wagler

Enchilada Casserole

1 lb. ground beef, fried and drained	1 16-oz. can refried beans
7 10-inch flour tortillas	1 4-oz. can chopped green chilies
1 8-oz. jar taco sauce	1 c. sour cream
1 large chopped onion	1 large chopped pepper
2 c. shredded cheddar cheese	2 c. shredded mozzarella cheese
1 2½-oz. can sliced ripe olives, drained	1 8-oz. can enchilada sauce
	extra cheese on top

Place one tortilla in a 12-inch round casserole dish. Layer ½ of taco sauce, beef, onion, and cheddar cheese. Add second tortilla. Press gently; layer ½ of beans, olives, and chilies. Third layer: tortilla, ½ of sour cream, green pepper, and mozzarella cheese. Fourth: tortilla, rest of beef, taco sauce, onion, and cheddar. Fifth: tortilla, beans, olives, and chilies. Sixth: tortilla, sour cream, pepper, and mozzarella cheese. Seventh: tortilla. Spread with enchilada sauce. Bake at 350° for 1 hour. Let stand a few minutes before cutting. Sprinkle with extra cheese if desired. Serves 10-12.

Mrs. Dewayne (Edna Sue) Miller

Enchilada Casserole

4 lb. ground beef	4 cans Rotel's tomatoes
1 10½-oz. can cream of mushroom soup	or 2 pt. salsa (Rotel's may be too spicy for some)
1 10½-oz. can tomato soup	4 c. crushed corn chips
10 corn or flour tortillas	3 to 4 c. shredded Colby Jack cheese
3 cans refried beans	

Brown beef; drain. Add both cans of soup and mix well. Spread into a large, well-greased casserole dish. Tear corn tortillas into bite-sized pieces and spread evenly over meat. Cook beans in saucepan, adding a little water to make smooth. Spread over tortillas. Next layer is Rotel's tomatoes or salsa. Break up corn chips and sprinkle over tomatoes. Add shredded cheese to top. Bake at 350° until cheese is golden and bubbly, about 45 minutes. This portion size fills a large roaster.

Mrs. Gregory (Denise) Rich

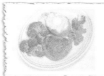

The quality of life is in the mind, not in material.

Biscuit and Taco Casserole

½ lb. ground beef
½ c. dairy sour cream
⅓ c. Miracle Whip dressing
1 T. chopped onion

½ c. shredded cheddar cheese
1 c. Bisquick biscuit mix
¼ c. cold water
1 pt. chunky salsa

Cook beef until browned; drain. Mix sour cream, dressing, onion, and cheese. Mix Bisquick and water until soft dough forms. Pat in greased 8 x 8-inch pan, pressing ½ inch up sides. Layer beef and salsa in pan; spoon sour cream mixture over top. Sprinkle with paprika or extra cheddar cheese over top. Bake at 375° for 25-30 minutes. You can substitute Bisquick with your favorite drop biscuit recipe. Mozzarella cheese is also good. Serves 5-6.

Mrs. Reuben (Elizabeth) Luthy

Mexican Chicken Roll-Ups

2½ c. cooked, deboned chicken
12 oz. sour cream
3 tsp. taco seasoning
1 can cream of mushroom soup

1½ c. shredded cheese
½ c. salsa
10 flour tortillas

In a bowl, combine chicken, ½ c. sour cream, 1½ tsp. taco seasoning, half of soup, 1 c. cheese, and salsa. Place ⅓ c. filling on each tortilla. Roll up and place seam-side down in a greased 9 x 13-inch baking dish. Combine remaining sour cream, taco seasoning, and soup. Pour over tortillas. Cover and bake at 350° for 30 minutes. Sprinkle with remaining cheese. Serve with additional salsa, chopped lettuce, and chopped tomatoes. Very delicious! Serves 15.

Marilyn R. Hershberger

A gossiper is like an old shoe—
its tongue never stays in place.

. . .

An unloving and critical spirit
is clear evidence that there is
something wrong inside.

Easy Taco Bake

1 lb. ground beef
½ c. chopped green pepper
½ c. chopped onions
8 corn tortillas
2 c. shredded mozzarella
   or other cheese
2 c. sour cream

1 pkg. taco seasoning
¾ c. water
½ c. Miracle Whip dressing
1 pt. jar salsa
2 c. chopped lettuce
1 c. chopped tomatoes

Brown beef, pepper, and onions. Fry until tender; add 1 pkg. taco seasoning and ¾ c. water. Simmer, then add dressing and salsa. Layer corn tortillas in bottom and sides of baking dish. Layer meat mixture on top, then cheese. Bake ½ hour until it's hot and cheese melts. To serve, layer sour cream, chopped lettuce, and tomatoes on top. Serves 8.

Mrs. John (Loma) Kauffman
Mrs. Orlie (Mary) Troyer

Spanish Rice

1 c. rice
1 lb. hamburger
1 onion
½ c. green peppers, diced

½ c. grated cheese
½ tsp. chili powder
salt and pepper to taste
tomato juice

Cook rice until soft. Brown hamburger and onion. Mix well with rest of ingredients. Spoon into 1½-qt. casserole dish. Cover with tomato juice. Bake for 1 hour at 350°. Serves 4-6.

Mrs. Ben (Keturah) Troyer

Baked Beans

1 lb. navy beans
½ lb. bacon (cut fine)
½ c. ketchup
1 medium onion

1½ T. salt
1 c. brown sugar
½ c. white sugar
1 pt. tomato juice

Soak beans overnight, then boil until tender. Drain off most of water and put in rest of ingredients. Bake 2½-3 hours at 350°. Do not cover.

Mrs. Perry (Delores) Herschberger

Baked Corn

2 c. corn
2 T. butter
1½ T. flour
1 c. milk

1 T. sugar
½ tsp. pepper
2 eggs, beaten

Butter casserole dish. Mix corn, flour, milk, sugar, pepper, and eggs. Dot with butter. Bake at 350° for 1 hour.

Mrs. Ben (Anna Mary) Fisher

Bar-B-Q Green Beans

½ lb. bacon
4 c. green beans
¾ tsp. salt
¼ c. onion, chopped

½ c. sugar
¾ c. ketchup
¾ tsp. Worcestershire sauce

Cut bacon in small pieces. Fry bacon and onion. Mix together and bake 1 hour at 300°. Serves 6.

Ruth Wengerd

Zucchini Casserole

3 c. zucchini, raw and grated
   (If peelings are tender, I leave
    them on.)
½ c. vegetable oil
½ c. grated cheese

4 eggs
½ onion
salt and pepper to taste
1 c. Bisquick, or 1 c. flour and
   1 tsp. baking powder

Beat vegetable oil with eggs, then add other ingredients. Bake uncovered at 350° until golden brown and firm. If you don't have cheese, it's very good with chicken gravy on top.

Alma Bontrager

It's a great thing doing little things well.

Chicken Dressing

1 20-oz. loaf of bread, cubed	⅛ tsp. pepper
1 qt. chicken broth	4 eggs
2 T. chicken seasoning	1½ c. milk
1 tsp. salt	1½ c. water
2 T. celery flakes	½ c. melted butter

In a large bowl, beat eggs; combine all the rest of the ingredients except bread. Mix well. Add bread and gently mix; pour into greased 4-qt. casserole dish. Bake at 350° for 1 hour.

Mrs. Omer (Martha) Miller

Shepherd's Pie

hamburger	Velveeta cheese
cream of mushroom soup	a little milk
onion	Hidden Valley Ranch dressing mix,
mashed potatoes	dry
sour cream	

Fry onion and hamburger. Put in bottom of a roaster. Add soup and milk and cover with cheese. Top with potatoes mashed with sour cream and dressing. Cover with cheese. Soup rises to top while baking.

Mrs. James (Rosanna) Miller

Ham and Potato Casserole

1 8-qt. kettle potatoes, cooked and shredded

6 c. ham	1 2-lb. box Velveeta cheese
Sauce:	
⅔ c. melted butter	1½ qt. milk
¼ tsp. pepper	2 10½-oz. cans cream of
1½ tsp. salt	chicken soup
1½ c. sour cream	

Whip sauce ingredients with wire whisk. Layer into 8-qt. casserole dish in this order: sauce, cheese, potatoes, and ham.

Mrs. Jerome (Rose) Graber

Tater Tot Casserole

1 lb. hamburger, browned
  and seasoned
1½ c. cooked mixed vegetables
1 can cream of chicken soup

1 can milk
cheese
1 lb. Tater Tots

Put the browned hamburger and mixed vegetables in a 2-qt. casserole dish. Dilute the soup with the milk and pour over the layers of meat and vegetables. Cover with cheese slices and top with frozen Tater Tots. Cover and bake 1¼ hours at 350°. Serves 6.

Ruby W. Mast

Potato Patch Casserole

1 lb. hamburger
½ c. chopped onion
1 egg
¼ c. milk
¼ c. bread crumbs
1 tsp. salt
¼ tsp. celery salt

½ tsp. black pepper
2 T. butter
1⅓ c. milk
1¼ tsp. salt
½ lb. Velveeta cheese
4 c. cooked potatoes
10 oz. frozen carrots, thawed

Combine hamburger, onion, egg, milk, bread crumbs, and seasonings. Shape into balls, roll in flour, and brown in skillet. Set aside. Make a white sauce with butter, milk, and salt; add cheese. Place potatoes and carrots in a 3- or 4-qt. casserole dish. Put meatballs on top and cover with sauce. Cover and bake at 350° for 1 hour.

Mrs. Noah (Fannie) Yoder

God does not give each one of us identical circumstances. But He gives each one of us His grace abundantly, no limit.

Potato Haystack Casserole

8 to 10 medium potatoes, cooked, peeled, and shredded
2 pkg. Buttermilk Hidden Valley Ranch dressing mix
1 c. sour cream
1 c. milk
4 lb. hamburger
1 to 2 pkg. (or 3 T.) taco seasoning
salt and pepper to taste
onion

Add sour cream and milk to dressing mix. Fry hamburger with onion and add taco seasoning. Layer all ingredients in casserole dish in order given, then put cheese sauce on top. Bake until hot. Before serving put crushed nacho chips on top.

Mrs. John (Carolyn) Otto

Cheesy Potato Bake

4 large unpeeled baking potatoes
¼ c. butter or margarine
1 T. grated onion
¾ tsp. salt
⅛ tsp. pepper
1 c. (4-oz.) shredded cheddar cheese
1 T. chopped fresh parsley

Thinly slice potatoes and place in a shallow, greased 2-qt. baking dish. In a small saucepan, heat butter, onion, salt, and pepper until butter is melted. Drizzle over potatoes. Cover with foil and bake at 425° for 45 minutes or until tender. Sprinkle with cheese and parsley. Bake uncovered 15 minutes longer or until the cheese melts. Serves 6-8.

Mrs. Jerome (Rose) Graber

Scalloped Potatoes

8 qt. potatoes
2 cans cream of chicken soup
1½ qt. milk
1½ c. sour milk
2 tsp. onion salt
¼ tsp. pepper
⅔ c. melted butter
1½ tsp. salt
1 box cheese

Layer in roaster and bake at 350° for 1 hour or until tender.

Mrs. Joe (Susie) Delagrange

Potluck Potatoes

5 lb. potatoes, peeled
1 c. butter
½ c. onion, chopped
1 c. flour
3 tsp. salt

½ tsp. black pepper
1 tsp. paprika
8 c. milk
1 lb. Velveeta cheese
1 to 2 c. sour cream

Cook potatoes until fairly soft; shred or slice. Melt butter; add onion and sauté for 5 minutes. Add flour and seasonings. Gradually add milk; cook and stir until thickened. Stir in cheese and sour cream and cover until cheese melts. Pour over potatoes and bake until heated through.

Mrs. Stephen (Amelia) Miller

Potluck Potatoes

2 lb. potatoes
1 10½-oz. can mushroom soup
2 c. Velveeta cheese

¼ tsp. pepper
1 pt. sour cream
1 tsp. Lawry's seasoning salt

Cook potatoes until almost soft. Peel and slice. Combine rest of ingredients and heat until cheese is melted. Layer potatoes and sauce in baking dish. Bake at 350° for 45 minutes. Top with crushed potato chips.

Irma Troyer

Party Potatoes

12 c. water
2 tsp. salt
5 tsp. onion salt
2 sticks butter

16 oz. cream cheese
2 c. sour cream
4½ c. milk
12 c. instant potato flakes

Bring first 4 ingredients to a boil, then turn off heat. Add next 4. These mashed potatoes are very good; you cannot tell they are instant. It is handy to fix for a large group. They can be made a day or 2 ahead of time. Put in a roaster and bake in a 350° oven until heated through or heat in a crockpot on medium for 2-3 hours. Stir occasionally. Serves 20-24.

Mrs. Roy (Martha) Hershberger

Frankfurter Bake

1 8-oz. pkg. noodles	½ tsp. salt
1¼ c. grated cheese	1 lb. wieners, sliced
1 c. milk	¼ c. brown sugar
¼ c. margarine	¼ c. Miracle Whip dressing
2 T. flour	1 T. mustard

In large kettle, cook noodles. Drain and return to kettle. Stir in sauce made from margarine, flour, milk, cheese, and salt. Pour into 12 x 13-inch baking dish, which is well greased. Spoon mixture of weiners, brown sugar, dressing, and mustard evenly over noodles. Bake 25 minutes at 375°. An excellent dish to take to school for hot lunch! The children's favorite! Serves 6.

Deborah Slabaugh

Yumasetti

1½ lb. hamburger	1½ c. cream of chicken soup
1½ c. cream of tomato soup	1 c. celery, cut up fine,
½ lb. Velveeta cheese	cooked until tender
1 pkg. wide noodles	salt and pepper to taste

Fry hamburger. Cook noodles until tender but not soft. Mix tomato soup with hamburger, and chicken soup with noodles. Put in layers with cheese in casserole dish. (You can also use pizza sauce instead of tomato soup for a delicious flavor.) Bake at 325° for 1 hour or until heated through.

Mrs. Nathan (Mattie) Miller

Salsa Mac-N-Cheese

1 lb. ground beef	2 c. elbow macaroni, uncooked
1 16-oz. jar chunky salsa	¾ lb. (12-oz.) Velveeta cheese, cut up
1¾ c. water	(I use less cheese.)

Brown meat in large skillet. Add salsa and water. Bring to boil. Stir in macaroni. Reduce heat to medium low; cover with tight-fitting lid. Simmer 8-10 minutes or until macaroni is tender. Add Velveeta and stir until melted. Serves 6.

Mrs. Wilbur (Joann) Hochstetler

Sloppy Joes

1½ lb. hamburger
1½ tsp. salt
¾ c. rolled oats
1 c. milk

1 c. catsup
½ c. water
2 T. sugar
2 T. vinegar

Mix and brown first four ingredients, then mix catsup, water, sugar, and vinegar and pour over the hamburger mix. Bake for 1 hour at 350°. Fills 15 regular size buns. Note: This sauce can be used on canned chunked beef too.

Ruby W. Mast

Pizza Sandwiches

6 to 8 slices bread
1 pt. pizza sauce
  Toppings:
mushrooms, pepperoni, peppers, onions, cheese, etc.

½ to 1 lb. hamburger or sausage

Lay bread on cookie sheet or pizza pan. Brown meat with onions; mix pizza sauce into meat; spoon onto bread; add toppings. Bake at 400° for 8-10 minutes.

Mrs. Wilbur (Joann) Hochstetler

Pizza Cups

1 pt. pizza sauce
1 lb. hamburger or sausage

1 can Pillsbury biscuits
1 pkg. mozzarella cheese

Brown and drain meat. Stir in pizza sauce. Cook over low heat for 5 minutes. Place biscuits in a greased muffin tin, pressing to cover bottom and sides. Spoon about ¼ c. meat mixture into each biscuit-lined cup; sprinkle with cheese. Bake at 350° for 10 minutes or until golden brown. Makes approximately 12 cups.

Mrs. Jr. (Esther) Wengerd

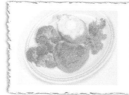

Lord, You know how busy I will be today; if I forget You, please do not forget me.

BLT Pizza

Prepare your favorite dough and line pan. Spoon on a layer of pizza sauce. Sprinkle on mozzarella or provolone cheese and plenty of fried, crumbled bacon. Bake until done. As soon as removed from oven, spread with mayonnaise. Layer on shredded lettuce and diced tomatoes. Enjoy!

Mrs. John (Rosanna) Bowman

Fireside Supper

whole potatoes
carrots

several slices turkey bacon

Wash potatoes and scrub carrots. Wrap potatoes with 2 slices of turkey bacon. Place on pieces of aluminum foil; place carrots, cut into 2-inch pieces, on top. Wrap tightly; place on cookie sheet in 350° oven for 1½ hours.

Mrs. Omer (Martha) Miller

Feathery Light Dumplings

1 c. sifted pastry flour	2 T. shortening
1½ tsp. baking powder	⅓ c. milk
½ tsp. salt	1 egg, beaten

Sift flour, baking powder, and salt together in a bowl. Cut in shortening with pastry blender until mixture is crumbly. Pour in milk and egg. Mix only until flour is dampened. (Dough should be lumpy.) Drop by teaspoonful on top of boiling meat mixture. Cover tightly and steam 12 minutes without removing cover. Makes 6 fluffy dumplings. To double recipe, increase milk to ¾ c. and use only 1 egg. Double other ingredients. Use a wide, shallow pan to provide more surface on which to cook 12 large dumplings.

For wheat dumplings, decrease flour to ⅔ c. and add ⅓ c. whole wheat or graham flour to dry ingredients before cutting in shortening. These are special with veal stew.

For dessert dumplings with fruit and sauce, see Desserts section, page 162.

Lena Yoder

Mom's "Original" Bar-B-Q Sauce

3 c. water
3 c. vinegar
3 T. brown sugar
1 tsp. pepper
½ lb. butter
1 T. garlic salt

1 T. onion salt or minced onion
1 T. seasoned salt
2 T. salt
5 T. Worcestershire sauce
1 T. celery salt

Mix and boil all ingredients, and then soak chicken in it for a day. Use on chicken while grilling. Enough for 25 pieces.

Mrs. Wilbur (Joann) Hochstetler

Sally's Coating for Chicken

4 c. flour (white or wheat)
4 T. salt
3 T. paprika
2 tsp. garlic salt

2 tsp. onion salt
4 c. crushed soda crackers
2 T. sugar

Stir all ingredients together to mix well. Store in covered container. When ready to use, coat chicken with mixture and put in pans with some melted butter in them. Bake at 375° until done. If desired you may dip chicken in liquid first, like milk or buttermilk. Is also good on pork chops and fish.

Mary Ann Mast

Sausage Gravy

1 lb. sausage (unseasoned)
¾ tsp. salt
pepper, optional

3 T. flour
2 to 2½ c. milk

Brown sausage in skillet. Add salt, flour, and milk. Bring to a slow simmer and keep stirring until it thickens. Serve over biscuits or toast.

Mrs. Norman (Marlena) Miller

Life is fragile; handle with prayer.
Harold B. Lee

Smoke Brine for Turkey

1 c. Morton's Tender Quick   1½ gal. water
¼ c. liquid smoke   1 c. Morton's Sugar Cure

Put turkey in crock and cover with brine. Cover and let stand 24 hours or 3-4 days in a cool place. Then pour off sauce and pour 1 stick melted butter over bird. Wrap in foil and bake 6-7 hours at 350°.

Mrs. Mahlon (Wanita Kay) Bontrager

Bar-B-Q Sauce

1 pt. vinegar   1 T. pepper
1 lb. butter   2 T. Worcestershire sauce
3 T. salt (omit if chicken   1 to 2 oz. Accent seasoning
    was salted)

Boil everything together and put on chicken while grilling. Option: I usually cook chicken on stove top for 5-10 minutes with Bar-B-Q sauce before grilling. Makes enough sauce for 20 lb. or 6 chickens.

Mrs. Mahlon (Wanita Kay) Bontrager

Procrastination is the thief of time.
Edward Young

. . .

"And whatsoever ye do, do it heartily, as to the Lord, and not unto men."
Colossians 3:23

. . .

Life isn't fair, but God is!
William Donald Gough

Candies and Snacks

Jesu! Jesu! Brunn des Lebens!

Heironymus Annoni, 1697-1770

John Wyeth, 1770-1858

1. Je - su! Je - su! Brunn des Le - bens! Stell, ach stell Dich bei uns ein!
2. Bist Du mit - ten un - ter de - nen, Wel - che sich nach Dei-nem Heil
3. Samm-le die zer - streu-ten Sin - nen, Wehr der Flat - ter - haf - tig - keit,
4. Gib uns Au - gen, gib uns Oh - ren, Gib uns Her - zen, die Dir gleich;

Dass wir jetz - und nicht ver - ge - bens Wir - ken und bei - sam - men sein.
Mit ver - ein - tem Seuf-zen seh - nen, O, so sei auch un - ser Teil.
Lass uns Licht und Kraft ge - win - nen Zu der Chris - ten We - sen - heit.
Mach uns red - lich neu - ge - bo - ren, Herr, zu Dei - nem Him - mel-reich.

Du ver-heis - sest ja den Dei-nen, Dass Du wol - lest Wun-der tun,
Lehr uns sin - gen, lehr uns be - ten, Hauch uns an mit Dei-nem Geist,
O, Du Haupt der rech-ten Glie-der, Nimm uns auch zu sol-chen an;
Ach, ja! lehr uns Chris-ten wer-den, Chris - ten, die ein Licht der Welt,

Und in ih - nen willst er - schei-nen, Ach, er - füll's, er - füll's auch nun.
Dass wir vor den Va - ter tre - ten, Wie es kind - lich ist und heisst.
Bring das Ab - ge - wich-ne wie - der Auf die fro - he Him-mels-bahn.
Chris-ten, die ein Salz der Er - den, Ach, Herr! wie es Dir ge - fällt.

Scotch-a-Roos

1 c. sugar
1 c. corn syrup
1 c. peanut butter

6 c. Rice Krispies
2 c. butterscotch chips

Cook sugar and corn syrup together over medium heat until mixture boils. Remove from heat and stir in peanut butter. Pour over Rice Krispies. Press into 9 x 13-inch pan. Melt butterscotch chips and spread on top.

Ruby Chupp

Cathedral Windows

6 oz. chocolate chips
2 T. butter
1 egg

3 c. mini colored marshmallows
½ c. chopped nuts
1 c. flaked coconut

Melt chocolate chips and butter in a double boiler. Add beaten egg and let cool. Fold in marshmallows and nuts. Turn out on waxed paper covered with coconut. Form into 12 x 2½-inch roll. Wrap roll in waxed paper or foil and freeze. Slice to serve.

Mrs. David (Rhoda) Miller

Coconut Mounds

⅔ c. white sugar
1 c. minus 1 T. corn syrup
4 c. coconut

3 T. water
chocolate

Combine sugar, water and corn syrup in saucepan. Heat to boiling; add coconut. Drop by tsp. on waxed paper; chill. I roll them in balls after they are chilled. Dip in chocolate.

Regina Miller

Dodging work is the hardest work of all and yields the poorest returns.
Bertie Charles Forbes

Caramel Candy

2 c. light corn syrup
2 c. sugar
salt
½ c. butter

1⅔ c. cream
1 tsp. vanilla
½ c. chopped nuts

Cook syrup, sugar, and salt together until it forms into a ball when a teaspoon of mixture is dropped into a cup of cold water. Add butter and cream gradually so that it doesn't stop boiling. Cook until firm ball stage (248°), stirring constantly. Pour into buttered pan. Cut into pieces.

Ruth Maria Herschberger

Maple Balls

3 lb. powdered sugar
1 can sweetened condensed milk
½ lb. finely chopped nuts

½ lb. margarine
2 tsp. maple flavoring

Melt margarine; add other ingredients except nuts; knead well. Add nuts. Roll in balls, then chill. Dip in melted chocolate. Delicious!

Joanna Miller

Creamy Caramels or Turtles

2 c. cream
2 c. sugar
1 c. corn syrup
½ tsp. salt

⅓ c. margarine
½ tsp. vanilla
nuts or cashews
chocolate

Heat cream until warm. Take out one cup. Add sugar, corn syrup, and salt. Cook. Slowly add the 1 c. cream. Keep boiling; cook for 5 minutes. Add margarine, bits at a time. Cook until firm ball in cold water. Add vanilla. Let cool. Add nuts or cashews, then coat with chocolate.

Marjorie Mast

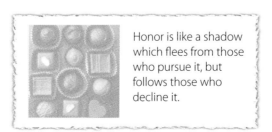

Honor is like a shadow which flees from those who pursue it, but follows those who decline it.

Cornflake Candy

1 c. white sugar
1 c. corn syrup
½ c. cream

4 c. cornflakes
1 c. shredded coconut
1 c. chopped nuts

Boil sugar, syrup, and cream until it reaches the soft ball stage. Pour over the rest. Mix well and pour into buttered pan.

Mrs. Dewayne (Edna Sue) Miller

Cornflake Candy

5 c. cornflakes
3 c. Rice Krispies
1 c. peanuts
1 c. sugar

1 c. light syrup
1 c. cream
1 tsp. vanilla

Boil together sugar, syrup, and cream until it forms a soft ball. Add vanilla. Pour over dry ingredients. Mix, then press into buttered pan.

Mrs. Norman (Marlena) Miller

Caramel Pecan Turtles

2 c. white sugar
¾ c. light corn syrup
1 c. cream
½ c. butter

1 c. cream
pecans
any desired chocolate coating

Cook and stir first 4 ingredients until mixture boils. Then add other cup of cream. Cook until it reaches soft ball stage or 238° on a candy thermometer. Place desired amount of pecans in 9-inch square pan. Pour caramel mixture over pecans. When cold, cut into 1-inch squares and dip into melted chocolate. Make sure that there's a complete seal or caramel will leak out. Yields approximately 3 lb.

Doris Yoder

Keep the truth, the Scripture truth, and it shall keep you.

. . .

Some people are so afraid to die that they never begin to live.

Henry van Dyke

Cinnamon Popcorn

10 to 13 qt. popped corn
1 c. sugar
1 c. Cinnamon Imperials
½ c. light corn syrup

1 tsp. salt
1 c. margarine
1 tsp. vanilla
½ tsp. baking soda

In heavy saucepan, boil margarine, sugar, syrup, Cinnamon Imperials, and salt for 5 minutes. Add vanilla and baking soda. Stir well. Pour over popcorn and mix well. Place on cookie sheets and bake 1 hour at 250°, stirring every 10-15 minutes. Store in tight container.

Mrs. Wilmer (Clara Mae) Yoder
Mrs. John (Carolyn) Otto

Oven Caramel Corn

3¾ qt. popped corn
1 c. brown sugar, packed
½ c. butter or margarine

¼ c. light corn syrup
½ tsp. salt
½ tsp. baking soda

Heat oven to 200°. Divide popped corn between 2 ungreased 9 x 13-inch baking pans. Heat sugar, butter, corn syrup, and salt, stirring occasionally, until bubbly around edges. Continue cooking over medium heat 5 minutes. Remove from heat. Stir in soda until foamy. Pour over popcorn, stirring until it is coated. Bake 1 hour, stirring every 15 minutes.

Mrs. John (Carolyn) Otto

Double-Decker Knox Blox Snacks

3 envelopes plain gelatin
3 pkg. (3 oz. each) flavored gelatin

2½ c. boiling water
1 c. heavy cream

Combine plain gelatin with flavored gelatin. Add boiling water; stir until dissolved. Stir in cream. Pour into shallow 9 x 9-inch baking pan. Chill until firm.

Emily Engbretson

If you don't have everything you want, be thankful for all the things you don't have that you don't want!

Granola Bars

¼ c. honey	4½ c. Rice Krispies
¾ c. margarine	5 c. rolled oats
¼ c. oil	1 c. coconut
½ c. peanut butter	1½ c. chocolate or butterscotch chips
1 tsp. vanilla	1 c. raisins, optional
20 oz. marshmallows	1 pkg. graham crackers, crushed

Cook first 5 ingredients together, heating until bottom is a wee bit burnt. Add marshmallows; stir until melted. Mix rest of ingredients together in bowl. Dump liquid mixture over this and mix and press into pan.

Rose Mary Miller

Granola Bars

2 10-oz. pkg. mini marshmallows	5 c. oatmeal
¼ c. honey	4½ c. Rice Krispies
¼ c. peanut butter	1 pkg. crushed graham crackers
¼ c. vegetable oil	1½ c. coconut
¾ c. butter	1 c. chocolate chips

Melt together the first 5 ingredients in a saucepan. In another bowl mix together the rest of the ingredients. Stir mixtures together and press into 2 cookie sheets. Cool.

Mrs. Orlie (Mary) Troyer
Amy Elizabeth Kauffman
Naomi Engbretson

Snack Mix Squares

2½ c. halved pretzel sticks	½ c. butter or margarine
2 c. Corn Chex	⅓ c. creamy peanut butter
1½ c. M&M's	5 c. miniature marshmallows

In a large bowl, combine pretzels, cereal, and M&M's. Melt butter and peanut butter in large saucepan over low heat. Add marshmallows; cook and stir until marshmallows are melted and mixture is smooth. Pour over pretzel mixture; stir to coat. Press into greased 9 x 13-inch pan. Cool until firm; cut into squares.

Mrs. Wilbur (Joann) Hochstetler

School Fuel

¾ c. packed brown sugar
6 T. margarine or butter
3 T. light corn syrup
¼ tsp. baking soda

4 c. Corn Chex cereal
4 c. Rice Chex cereal
¼ c. semisweet chocolate chips

Cover cookie sheet with waxed paper. Heat brown sugar, margarine, and corn syrup until margarine is melted. Stir in baking soda until dissolved. Stir in cereals. Bake at 250° for 30 minutes or until crisp, stirring every 15 minutes. Spread on cookie sheet. Cool 10 minutes; break into bite-size pieces. Melt chocolate chips. Drizzle chocolate over snack. Refrigerate 30 minutes or until chocolate is set. Store in airtight container. Makes 8 c.

Martha Graber
Amy Elizabeth Kauffman

Popcorn Balls

2 c. sugar
1 tsp. cream of tartar
½ c. water

1 T. butter
1 tsp. baking soda
6 qt. popped corn

Cook first 4 ingredients slowly until it turns brown. Add baking soda. Stir rapidly until well mixed. Pour mixture over popcorn. Shape into balls with buttered hands or leave as Cracker Jack.

Beth Ann Yoder

Best Ever Granola Bars

4½ c. Rice Krispies cereal
5 c. quick oats
1 c. coconut
1 pkg. graham crackers, crushed
1½ c. chocolate chips
1 c. raisins, optional

1 scant c. margarine or butter
¼ c. cooking oil
¼ c. honey
½ c. peanut butter
1 tsp. vanilla
2 10-oz. pkg. mini marshmallows

In a large greased bowl, mix all the dry ingredients together. Melt margarine over low heat; add oil, honey, peanut butter, and vanilla; melt all together. Add marshmallows and stir until melted. Pour immediately over dry ingredients in bowl and mix. Pat into a very well-greased 10 x 15-inch cookie sheet. Cut into bars. Yields 32 bars.

Anna Yoder

Chocolate Granola Bars

1 c. light corn syrup
½ c. white sugar
1 heaping T. peanut butter
2 c. Rice Krispies

4 c. rolled oats
½ c. chocolate chips
½ c. mixed nuts

Put corn syrup and sugar in saucepan and bring to a boil. Add peanut butter and stir until melted. In a large bowl, mix the other 4 ingredients. Pour on the hot mixture and blend all together. Press into a greased 9 x 13-inch pan. Enjoy!

Mrs. Jerry (Ruth) Gingerich

Muddy Buddies

9 c. Chex cereal
1 6-oz. pkg. chocolate chips
½ c. peanut butter

¼ c. margarine or butter
1 tsp. vanilla
1½ c. powdered sugar

Measure cereal into large bowl; set aside. Heat chocolate chips, peanut butter, and margarine in 1-qt. saucepan over low heat, stirring frequently until melted. Remove from heat; stir in vanilla. Pour chocolate mixture over cereal, stirring until evenly coated. Pour into large plastic food-storage bag; add powdered sugar. Seal bag; shake until well coated. Spread onto waxed paper to cool. Store in airtight container in refrigerator. Makes 9 cups of snack.

Martha Graber

Ranch Pretzels

¾ c. vegetable oil
1 pkg. ranch dressing mix
½ tsp. dill weed

½ tsp. lemon pepper
½ tsp. garlic salt

Mix together and pour over 30 oz. of pretzels. Bake for 30 minutes at 250°, stirring every 10 minutes.

Martha Graber

A friend is someone who goes around saying nice things about you behind your back.

Ranch Pretzels

1 c. oil
1 pkg. ranch dressing mix

2 T. dill weed
2 lb. pretzels

Mix all together in large mixing bowl. Stir every so often for 2 hours. Pour out onto large cookie sheets to dry.

Rachel Wengerd

Sour Cream and Onion Crackers

1 lb. white crackers
1 c. salad oil

3 T. sour cream and onion powder

Put crackers in Fix N Mix bowl. Mix salad oil and sour cream and onion powder. Pour over crackers and shake. Put in roaster and bake 20 minutes at 250°.

Mary Ann Mast

No one ever hardened his heart against God and prospered.

. . .

There is no right way to do a wrong deed.

Canning and Freezing

Joy to the World

Rejoice greatly, O daughter of Zion. —Zechariah 9:9

From Psalm 98
Isaac Watts, 1674-1748

Arr. from George F. Handel, 1685-1759

Chicken Bologna

1 lb. Tender Quick
30 lb. meat (cut off bones)
1 oz. black pepper
½ c. brown sugar
2 tsp. saltpeter

2 lb. fine cracker crumbs
4 rounded T. chicken base
3 T. liquid smoke
1 gal. water

Grind meat and mix in Tender Quick; let set 24 hours. Mix in rest of ingredients. Pressure can 1 hour at 10 lb. pressure or cold pack 2 hours.

Mrs. James (Rosanna) Miller

Homemade Bologna

100 lb. ground beef or venison
2 oz. black pepper
1 lb. brown sugar
3 lb. Tender Quick

2 T. red pepper
1½ oz. ground coriander
1 oz. mace
30 lb. cold water (approx. 3½ gallons)

Mix seasonings together in a bowl. Sprinkle evenly over ground meat and mix thoroughly with hands. Add 30 lb. water and mix well into meat. Leave set for 3-4 days in a cold place. Grind it once more and then pack tightly into jars. Process in a hot water bath for 3 hours, or in a pressure cooker at 10 lb. pressure for 90 minutes.

Mrs. Freeman (Wilma) Troyer

Beef or Venison Bologna

50 lb. fresh meat, ground
2 tsp. garlic powder
1 T. saltpeter

4 T. black pepper
1½ lb. Tender Quick
1 tsp. liquid smoke, optional

Mix well. Let set for 3-4 days. Put in jars and process.

Mrs. Kenneth (Martha) Miller

It isn't enough to be busy. What are you busy about?

Bologna

40 lb. fresh pork	1 lb. salt
60 lb. fresh beef	3 oz. mace
3 oz. pepper	5 lb. rolled oats
5 c. brown sugar	3 T. garlic salt
4 lb. Tender Quick	10 lb. water (approx. 1.2 gallons)

Grind pork and beef, then mix all together. Let stand 4 days. Grind again, stuff in cloth or casing, and smoke. Or you can pack in jars and add liquid smoke to suit taste. (I put ¾ tsp. to a qt. smoking, or liquid smoke is optional.) Cook for 3 hours in hot water bath. Makes around 50 qt.

Mrs. Joe (Susie) Delagrange

Bologna

60 lb. beef	1 oz. coriander
40 lb. pork	1½ oz. mace
3 lb. Tender Quick	4 drops liquid smoke
3 oz. black pepper	to each lb. meat
1½ to 2 oz. garlic powder	

Mix Tender Quick with meat and grind coarsely; let stand overnight. Then grind again fine. Add seasoning and mix well. Add 6-7 qt. water to meat. We usually put our liquid smoke in the water, then add to meat. Can use all beef or pork. I use any kind of meat in this recipe. Very good!

Alma Bontrager

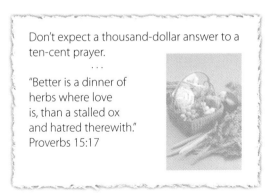

Don't expect a thousand-dollar answer to a ten-cent prayer.

. . .

"Better is a dinner of herbs where love is, than a stalled ox and hatred therewith."
Proverbs 15:17

Barbecued Meatballs

3 lb. ground meat (beef)
1 12-oz. can evaporated milk
1 c. oatmeal
1 c. cracker crumbs
2 eggs
   Sauce:
2 c. catsup
1 c. brown sugar
½ tsp. liquid smoke or to taste

½ c. chopped onions
½ tsp. garlic powder
2 tsp. salt
½ tsp. pepper
2 tsp. chili powder

½ tsp. garlic powder
¼ c. chopped onion

To make meatballs, combine all ingredients. (Mixture will be soft.) Shape into walnut-size balls. Place meatballs in a single layer on wax paper-lined cookie sheets. Freeze until solid. Store frozen meatballs in freezer bags until ready to cook. To make sauce, combine all ingredients and stir until sugar is dissolved. Place frozen meatballs in a 9 x 13-inch baking pan; pour on sauce. Bake at 350° for 1 hour. Yields 80 meatballs.

Alma Bontrager

Sandwich Spread

6 red peppers
6 green peppers
6 large pickles
6 green tomatoes
6 onions
6 carrots
10 stalks celery

½ c. salt
¾ pt. vinegar
1¼ pt. water
5 c. sugar
1 T. turmeric
1 qt. prepared mustard
1 c. flour

Grind vegetables, mix together, and add salt and a little water. Let stand 2 hours; drain and add vinegar and water. Cook 20 minutes. Add remaining ingredients and cook 5 minutes more, stirring constantly. Put in jars and cold pack 10 minutes. Yields 20-25 pints.

Mrs. Monroe (Elsie) Miller

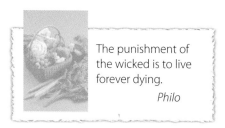

The punishment of the wicked is to live forever dying.

Philo

Pork Sausage

65 lb. ground pork	5 c. brown sugar
1 c. salt	1 c. liquid smoke
5 T. pepper	

Mix well.

Mrs. Leroy (Viola) Mast

Bean and Bacon Soup (to can)

4 lb. dried navy beans	salt to taste
2 lb. bacon	8 c. potatoes
6 c. onion, cut up	4 qt. tomato juice
4-6 c. celery	4 c. carrots
2 tsp. pepper	2 bay leaves

Soak navy beans overnight, then cook until real soft. Cook potatoes, carrots, and celery until good and soft. Cut bacon fine and fry. Remove bacon and cook onion in bacon grease until soft. Put all ingredients together in canner; heat until it simmers. Remove bay leaves before putting in jars. Makes about 16 qt. Process for 90 minutes at 10 lbs. pressure.

Mrs. James (Rosanna) Miller

Chili (to can)

10 lb. hamburger	3 c. flour
1 tsp. red pepper	4 qt. ketchup
6 tsp. salt	2 c. brown sugar
2 rounded T. chili powder	10 qt. water
1 c. chopped onions	1 gal. canned pork & beans

Fry hamburger, seasonings, and onions together. Mix together flour and brown sugar; add water. When it starts to thicken, add ketchup, beans, and hamburger. Cook until hot. Process 90 minutes at 10 lb. pressure.

Mrs. John (Carolyn) Otto

Vegetable Beef Soup (to can)

1¼ c. beef soup base
2 large cans beef broth
6 qt. tomato juice
2 qt. pizza sauce
2 large onions
3 qt. peas
1 qt. celery
4 qt. potatoes
4 qt. carrots
8 lb. seasoned fried hamburger

4 lb. cooked beef roast
1½ c. browned butter
2 qt. water
2 28-oz. cans Bush's pork & beans
5 c. Perma-flo
2 c. brown sugar
¼ scant c. salt
beef base
2 gal. water

In a 12-qt. kettle, thicken last 5 ingredients. In a large bowl, add the rest of ingredients. Save time by putting potatoes and carrots through the Salad Master. Mix thickened mixture with all ingredients. Put in jars. Process 75 minutes at 10 lb. pressure. Makes 30 qt.

Mrs. Omer (Martha) Miller

Zucchini Soup

3 qt. diced zucchini
2 c. chopped onion
4 tsp. salt

2 c. water
2 T. chicken base

Cook all ingredients until tender, then put through a blender. (I used a Salsa Master.) To can, use 10 lb. pressure for 25 minutes.

To make soup:

2 T. butter
2 c. milk

2 T. flour

Melt butter and add flour and milk. Cook until thickened, then add soup.

Mrs. Elvie (Rebekah) Miller

Of all the commentaries on the Scriptures, good examples are the best.

John Donne

Canned Tomato Soup

8 qt. cut up tomatoes
12 small onions, chopped
½ bunch celery, chopped
½ pkg. carrots, chopped
fresh parsley to taste

¼ c. salt
½ c. sugar
¼ c. flour
¼ tsp. cayenne pepper

Cook vegetables thoroughly and strain. (I put mine through a ricer or food mill.) Bring to a boil; make a paste of salt, sugar, flour, and pepper mixed with a little cold water. Add to hot mixture, stirring constantly. Add 2 T. lemon juice or ½ tsp. citric acid to each quart jar and then ladel in the soup, leaving ½-inch headspace, and process in boiling water bath for 40 minutes To serve, heat soup and equal amount of milk in separate saucepans. Add pinch of baking soda to soup, then add hot milk and a pat of butter.

Mrs. Stephen (Amelia) Miller

Catsup

1 gal. tomato juice
4 c. sugar
2 c. vinegar

2 T. salt
2 T. cinnamon
2 small onions

Combine all ingredients except onions and cinnamon. Put onions and cinnamon in cloth bag. Cook until thick enough. (Thickener can be added.)

Mrs. Perry Herschberger

Catsup

1 bunch tomatoes
5 green or red peppers
5 stalks celery
5 large onions
½ gal. vinegar

8 to 9 c. sugar
½ c. salt
1 T. celery seed
2 T. mixed pickling spice
1 T. allspice

Cook together tomatoes, peppers, celery, and onions, then run through strainer. Put juice in pillowcase. Let drip overnight or a few hours. Take pulp from bag and cook with rest of ingredients. Put spices in cloth bag before adding. Simmer 20 minutes. Put in jars and seal. (A method I like better is to add tomato paste to thicken instead of putting in pillowcase to drain.) Makes approximately 40 pt.

Mrs. Monroe (Elsie) Miller

The Authentic Amish Cookbook

Fruity Chili Sauce

20 medium tomatoes, chopped	1 sweet red pepper, chopped
6 medium onions, chopped	4 c. sugar
5 ripe peaches, peeled and chopped	1 c. vinegar
5 ripe pears, chopped	2 T. salt
1 green pepper, chopped	¼ c. mixed pickling spices

In a large kettle, combine all ingredients except the spices; bring to a boil. Reduce heat to simmer. Tie pickling spices in a double thickness of cheesecloth; add to tomato mixture. Simmer uncovered for 1½ hours or until volume is reduced by half, stirring frequently. Discard spice bag. Stores in refrigerator up to 2 months or ladle hot into hot jars, leaving ¼-inch headspace. Adjust caps. Process for 15 minutes in a boiling water bath. Serve over cooked pork, chicken, or turkey. Yields about 8 pt.

Mrs. Stephen (Amelia) Miller
Mrs. David (Rhoda) Miller

Tomato Soya

1 peck ripe tomatoes, peeled and diced	2 lb. brown sugar
	½ c. salt
8 onions, diced	1 tsp. ginger
1 pt. vinegar	1 tsp. mustard
1 tsp. cinnamon	½ tsp. black pepper
1 tsp. cloves	

Chop tomatoes and onions; add salt. Let stand overnight. Pour into colander and drain off juice; pour water over it and drain again. Add rest of ingredients except sugar. Cook slowly for 2 hours; add brown sugar. Put in pint jars. Cold pack for 15 minutes. Real good on meats, especially roasts.

Mrs. John (Loma) Kauffman

The Christian is not ruined by living in the world, but by the world living in him.

. . .

Circumstances make us neither strong nor weak; they just show which we are.

Pizza Sauce

½ bunch tomatoes
3 lb. onions
2 green peppers
3 hot peppers
2 whole garlic cloves
1½ c. sugar

½ c. salt
2 c. vegetable oil
4 8-oz. cans tomato sauce
2 T. basil
2 T. oregano
6 bay leaves

Cook tomatoes, onions, green peppers, hot peppers, and garlic and drain through sieve. Add other ingredients. Cook 1 hour or until thick, and then can. I use ½ tsp. garlic powder instead of whole garlic.

Mrs. Jerome (Rose) Graber

Taco Sauce

8 qt. tomatoes, chopped
1½ c. hot peppers, chopped
3 c. green peppers, chopped
6 medium onions, chopped
5 large cloves garlic, minced
3 cilantro leaves

1 c. sugar
⅓ c. vinegar
½ c. salt
3 T. chili powder
3 tsp. oregano
1 tsp. cumin

Mix all together; boil slowly for 2 hours. Ladle into jars and seal. Makes 12 pt.

Mrs. Michael (Lydia Ann) Stoll

Zucchini Relish

12 c. shredded zucchini
4 c. finely chopped onions
4 c. finely shredded cabbage
2 red sweet peppers, chopped
2 green sweet peppers, chopped
5 T. salt
6 c. sugar

2½ c. vinegar
5 T. cornstarch
1 T. dry mustard
1½ tsp. celery seed
1 tsp. turmeric
½ tsp. nutmeg
½ tsp. pepper

Mix zucchini, onions, cabbage, peppers, and salt well. Let stand overnight. Rinse well with cold water; drain. Combine rest of ingredients in saucepan and cook until slightly thickened. Add vegetables and mix well. Fill jars. Cold pack for 15 minutes.

Mrs. Steve (Edith) Engbretson

Zucchini Relish

10 c. chopped zucchini	2 tsp. turmeric
4 c. chopped onions	2 tsp. black pepper
1 chopped green pepper	2 tsp. celery seed
6 T. salt	1 T. mustard seed
4 c. sugar	2 tsp. nutmeg
2 c. vinegar	10 whole cloves
1 T. flour	(or 1 tsp. ground cloves)

Mix together first four ingredients and let stand overnight. Rinse and drain. Put in large kettle and add the rest of the ingredients. Bring to boil and cook for about 25 minutes. Pack in hot jars and seal. Makes approximately 7 pt.

Mrs. Kenneth (Martha) Miller

Zucchini Relish

10 c. unpeeled zucchini, shredded or coarsely ground	4 c. peppers (2 red and 2 green for color)
4 c. chopped onions	1 tsp. nutmeg
5 T. salt	1 tsp. dry mustard
1 tsp. black pepper	1 tsp. turmeric
2¼ c. vinegar	1 tsp. celery seed
	4 c. sugar

Mix zucchini, onions, and salt and let stand overnight. Next day drain mixture and rinse twice. Add the rest of ingredients. Cook 30 minutes. Put in jars while hot and seal.

Mrs. John Almon (Elmina) Mast

Easy Pickles

1 tsp. celery seed	3 c. vinegar
1 tsp. mustard seed	6 c. sugar
1 tsp. salt	1 tsp. turmeric
3 c. water	

Put first 3 ingredients in bottom of jar and then fill with sliced pickles. Heat remaining ingredients; when dissolved pour over pickles. Cold pack 5 minutes.

Mrs. Steve (Edith) Engbretson

Sour Dill Pickles

3 qt. water	dill
1 qt. vinegar	garlic
1 c. salt	cucumbers

Into a qt. jar, put a spray of dill and a clove of garlic. Fill jar with sliced cucumbers. Pour brine over cucumbers. Put in canner and bring to a boil. Remove from heat.

Mrs. Ben (Keturah) Troyer

Garlic Dill Pickles

2 c. vinegar	2 T. salt
2 c. water	garlic
3 c. sugar	dill
enough fresh pickles to fill 4 qt. jars	

Mix vinegar, water, sugar, and salt together and heat in saucepan. Wash pickles. Chunk or slice unpeeled pickles and pack tightly into quart jars. Add 2 garlic buds to each quart along with 1 head dill. Pour heated brine over pickles in jars and seal. Place jars in hot water bath and process only until the water comes to a full rolling boil. Turn off heat and remove jars from the water.

Mrs. Freeman (Wilma) Troyer

Freezer Pickles

2 qt. sliced cucumbers	3 tsp. salt
1 green pepper, sliced (optional)	1 onion, sliced
Syrup:	
½ c. white vinegar	½ tsp. celery seed
1½ c. sugar	

Mix first four ingredients together and soak in water for 2 hours. Drain. Mix syrup and set to dissolve while cucumbers are soaking. Put cucumbers in freezer containers; cover with syrup and freeze.

Mrs. Wilmer (Clara Mae) Yoder

Sweet Corn (to can)

1 bottle corn canning acid   ½ c. salt
   (available at E&R Seeds)   2 c. sugar
3 qt. warm water   20 qt. sweet corn

Mix acid, water, salt, and sugar. Put ⅔ c. into 20 qt. jars. Fill jars with sweet corn and process at 10 lb. pressure for 85 minutes. Almost as good as frozen sweet corn.

Mrs. Loyal (Dorcas) Gingerich

Pork and Beans (to can)

8 lb. dry navy beans   4 c. brown sugar
1½ lb. bacon   ½ tsp. red pepper
⅓ c. salt   1 tsp. cinnamon
4½ qt. tomato juice   1 large onion
1 qt. water   1½ large 26-oz. ketchup bottle
3 c. white sugar   (39 oz. altogether)

Fill pan halfway with beans and fill up with water; soak overnight. Next morning pour off water and put clean water on them. Cook until almost soft. Pour off water. Fry onion and bacon (cut in small squares) and add to beans, grease and all. Add the rest of ingredients and mix together. Put in jars and cold pack for 3 hours. Can be processed in pressure canner for 75 minutes at 10 lb. I doubled this and got 63 quarts. Is very good!

Alma Bontrager

Rhubarb (to can)

4 tsp. cornstarch   6 c. sugar
2 c. water   4 qt. rhubarb

Boil together water and cornstarch in 6-qt. kettle. Then add sugar and rhubarb. Boil until tender. Put in jars and seal. Strawberry Jell-O may be added for flavor.

Mrs. John (Fannie) Miller

Apple Pie Filling (to can)

water
3 c. white sugar
3 c. brown sugar
1 T. cinnamon
1 tsp. cloves

½ c. lemon juice
1 tsp. salt
Perma-flo
apples

Fill 10-qt. saucepan ¾ full of water. Add next 6 ingredients. Mix Perma-flo with water, enough to thicken the above mixture. I pour this into a 13-qt. mixing bowl and add enough apples that have been shredded (I use the King Cutter, cone number 3). This fills a 13-qt. mixing bowl. Cold pack 15 minutes.

Mrs. Dan (Mary) Miller

Grape Juice

For 2-qt. cans: put 3 cups grapes in can. Add 1 c. sugar. Fill with hot water and stir in sugar until dissolved. Put on lids and cold pack for 10 minutes.

Mrs. Loyal (Dorcas) Gingerich

Sugar Syrup for Canning and Freezing

Light syrup: 2 c. sugar and 4 c. water; yields 5 c.
Medium syrup: 3 c. sugar and 4 c. water; yields 5½ c.
Heavy syrup: 4¾ c. sugar and 4 c. water; yields 6½ c.

Heat sugar and water until sugar is dissolved. For canning, keep syrup hot until used, but don't boil down. For freezing, refrigerate until ice cold.

Mrs. James (Rosanna) Miller

Let Christ's beauty shine through me,
for all the whole world to see.
. . .
Greet the dawn with enthusiasm
and you may expect satisfaction at
sunset.

Desserts

I Thank the Lord My Maker

Giving thanks always for all things unto God. —Ephesians 5:20

Thomas MacKellar, 1812-1899

George J. Webb, 1803-1887

1. I thank the Lord my Mak-er For all His gifts to me; For mak-ing me par-
2. I thank the Lord my Sav-iour Who came for me to die, And bless me with His
3. I thank the Lord for giv-ing The Spir-it of His grace, That I may serve Him

tak - er Of boun-ties rich and free; For fa-ther and for moth-er, Who give me
fa - vor, And fit me for the sky, — That all my sins out-blot-ted, By Je-sus
liv - ing, And dy-ing, reach the place Where Je-sus in His glo - ry I shall for-

clothes and food, For sis - ter and for broth - er, And all the kind and good.
washed a - way, I may be found un-spot - ted When comes the fi - nal day.
ev - er see, And tell the won-drous sto - ry Of all His love for me.

Angel Food Icebox Cake

2 pkg. raspberry Jell-O
2½ c. water, boiled
1 c. sugar
2 pt. non-dairy topping

2 c. crushed pineapple
12 large marshmallows, cut fine
1 angel food cake

Pour boiling water over Jell-O and sugar; stir until dissolved. Chill until it starts to thicken. Beat well, then add topping beaten stiff. Add pineapple and marsh-mallows. Slice cake in thin slices into large pan. Arrange in layers of cake and Jell-O mixture. End with Jell-O on top. Place in refrigerator overnight. Can use strawberries instead of pineapple.

Marilyn Kay Herschberger

Apple Cream Cheese Pie

2 cans refrigerated biscuits,
    extra rich or buttermilk
2 pkg. cream cheese
½ c. sugar

2 tsp. vanilla
2 pt. apple pie filling
1 12-oz. can of caramel
1 c. chopped pecans

Roll out each biscuit until completely flat. Layer bottom of 9 x 13-inch pan and up the sides some too. Press in pan as a crust. Mix cream cheese, sugar, and vanilla together until well blended and spread over crust. Top with apple pie filling. Bake at 350° until crust is golden. Drizzle caramel and then sprinkle pecans over top. Enough for 2 pans.

Emily Engbretson

Grape Jell-O Dessert

4 c. whipped topping
⅔ c. grape Jell-O, dissolved
    in 2 c. hot water

¼ c. powdered sugar
8-oz. cream cheese
1 c. grapes

Beat together cream cheese and powdered sugar. Add whipped topping into cream cheese mixture. Add partly thickened Jell-O and grapes. Let set. Dissolve another ⅔ c. grape Jell-O in 2 c. hot water. Let cool then put onto the set Jell-O.

Mrs. Jerome (Rose) Graber

Rhubarb Torte

1 c. flour	1¼ c. sugar
2 T. sugar	2 T. flour
pinch of salt	3 egg yolks (save the whites)
½ c. butter or margarine	⅓ c. half and half
2¼ c. rhubarb	

Mix first four ingredients for crust; press into 8 x 10-inch pan and bake at 325° for 20-25 minutes. In a saucepan, combine rest of ingredients. Cook until thick; pour into baked crust. For topping, beat the egg whites, ¼ tsp. cream of tartar, and 6 T. sugar. Spread over rhubarb mixture. Brown in 325° oven for 10-15 minutes.

Mrs. Omer (Martha) Miller

Cranberry Fluff

3 c. coarsely chopped cranberries	⅛ tsp. salt
1 20-oz. can crushed pineapple, drained	¼ c. walnuts
	2 c. whipping cream
1 medium apple, peeled and chopped	or Rich's topping, beaten
2 c. mini marshmallows	8 oz. cream cheese
⅔ c. sugar	

Combine first 7 ingredients; mix well. Cover and refrigerate overnight. Just before serving, mix whipped cream and cream cheese together and fold in.

Mrs. Dan (Mary) Miller

Fluffy Mint Dessert

1-lb. pkg. cream-filled chocolate sandwich cookies, crushed	2 12-oz. cartons frozen whipped topping, thawed
2 c. pastel miniature marshmallows	1⅓ c. small pastel mints

Reserve ¼ c. of crushed cookies for garnish. Combine the remaining cookie crumbs with ½ c. melted butter; press into 9 x 13-inch pan. Fold together whipped topping, marshmallows, and mints; pour over crust. Garnish with reserved cookie crumbs. Cover and refrigerate at least 2 days before serving. Or may be frozen; allow to thaw before serving. Serves 18-20.

Mrs. Omer (Martha) Miller

Creamy Orange Fluff

1 6-oz. pkg. orange gelatin
2½ c. boiling water
2 11-oz. cans mandarin oranges,
    drained

1 8-oz. can crushed pineapple,
    undrained
1 6-oz. can frozen orange juice
    concentrate, thawed

Topping:
1 8-oz. pkg. cream cheese, softened
1 c. cold milk

1 3.4-oz. pkg. instant vanilla
    pudding mix

In a bowl, dissolve gelatin in boiling water. Stir in oranges, pineapple, and orange juice. Coat a 9 x 13-inch dish with nonstick cooking spray; add gelatin mixture. Refrigerate until firm. Beat cream cheese until light. Gradually add milk and pudding mix; beat until smooth. Spread over orange layer. Chill until firm. Serves 12-16.

Mrs. Wilbur (Joann) Hochstetler

Graham Cracker Fluff

2 egg yolks
½ c. sugar
⅔ c. milk
1 pkg. (1 T.) gelatin
½ c. cold water
2 egg whites

1 c. whipping cream
1 tsp. vanilla
3 T. melted butter
3 T. sugar
12 graham crackers

Beat egg yolks and add sugar and milk. Cook in top of double boiler until slightly thickened. Soak gelatin in the cold water. Pour hot mixture over softened gelatin and stir until smooth. Chill until slightly thickened. Add stiffly beaten egg whites, vanilla, and whipped cream to chilled mixture. Combine melted butter, cracker crumbs, and sugar to make crumbs. Sprinkle half of crumbs in bottom of serving dish. Add mixture and top with remaining crumbs. Let chill in refrigerator until set. Serves 6-8.

Mrs. Glen (Marilyn) Miller
Mrs. Alva (Elnora) Hochstetler

Jesus, friend of little children,
Be a friend to me:
Take my hand and ever keep me
Close to Thee.

Walter J. Mathams

Vanilla Pudding

⅓ c. all-purpose flour
⅔ c. packed brown sugar
2 c. milk
2 egg yolks, beaten
2 T. butter

1 tsp. vanilla
1 c. heavy cream, whipped
4 to 6 bananas
chopped walnuts

In a medium saucepan, combine the flour and brown sugar; stir in milk. Cook and stir over medium heat until thickened and bubbly. Cook and stir 1 minute more. Remove from heat. Gradually stir about 1 c. hot mixture into egg yolks. Return all to saucepan. Bring to a gentle boil; cook and stir 2 minutes. Remove from heat; stir in butter and vanilla. Cool to room temperature, stirring occasionally. Fold in whipped topping. Put pudding and bananas in layers. Sprinkle top with nuts if desired. Cover and chill 1 hour before serving. Good and not so rich pudding! Serves 6-8.

Mrs. Monroe (Elsie) Miller

Chocolate Cream Dessert

3 c. crushed vanilla wafers
⅔ c. butter or margarine, melted
  Filling:
1 7-oz. milk chocolate candy bar,
  plain or with almonds, broken
  into pieces
1 10-oz. pkg. large marshmallows

¼ c. sugar
½ tsp. ground cinnamon

1 c. milk
2 c. whipping cream, whipped
½ tsp. vanilla extract
sliced almonds, toasted, optional

In a bowl, combine wafer crumbs, butter, sugar, and cinnamon; mix well. Set aside ⅓ c. for topping. Press remaining crumb mixture into a greased 13 x 9-inch pan; refrigerate until firm. In a saucepan, heat the candy bar, marshmallows, and milk over medium-low heat until chocolate and marshmallows are melted, stirring often. Remove from heat; cool to room temperature. Fold in whipped cream and vanilla; pour over crust. Chill 3-4 hours. Sprinkle with reserved crumb mixture and almonds if desired. Serves 12-16.

Mrs. Jerome (Rose) Graber

Give others a piece
of your heart, not a
piece of your mind.

Chocolate Dessert

Crust:

1½ c. flour
¾ c. butter

Second Part:

8 oz. cream cheese
½ c. powdered sugar

Topping:

2 c. cold milk
1 box instant vanilla pudding

1 tsp. baking soda
1 c. chopped walnuts or pecans

1 c. Cool Whip

1 box instant chocolate pudding
Cool Whip

Mix crust and press in pan. Bake at 350° for 15-20 minutes. Cool. Mix second part and put on top of crust. Mix milk with pudding and then top with Cool Whip. Can also cook pudding either from scratch or the cook type bought in boxes.

Mrs. David (Rhoda) Miller

Delicious Delight

Crust:

2 c. flour
1 c. butter, melted

Second Layer:

1 c. powdered sugar

Third Layer:

2 3.4-oz. pkg. instant vanilla pudding mix

½ c. nuts

1 8-oz. container Cool Whip
1 8-oz. pkg. cream cheese

3 c. milk

Crust: Blend together and press into ungreased 9 x 13-inch pan. Bake at 350° for 15 minutes; cool. Second layer: Cream sugar and cream cheese; fold in Cool Whip. Pour over crust. Third layer: Mix and pour over cream cheese mixture. Top with Cool Whip.

Mrs. Jerome (Rose) Graber

You're not what you think you are; but what you THINK— you are!

Butterscotch Pudding

5½ c. milk, scalded
½ c. sugar
⅓ c. Clear Jel
½ tsp. salt
1 tsp. vanilla

2 eggs
½ c. milk
1 3-oz. box butterscotch pudding and
pie filling mix, cook type

Mix dry ingredients, beaten eggs, and ½ c. cold milk. Pour into hot milk and stir until it thickens. Add vanilla.

Irma Troyer

Coconut Crunch Delight

½ c. butter or margarine, melted
1 c. flour
1¼ c. flaked coconut
¼ c. packed brown sugar
1 3.4-oz. pkg. instant vanilla
pudding mix

1 3.4-oz. pkg. instant coconut
pudding mix
2⅔ c. cold milk
2 c. whipped topping
fresh strawberries, optional

In a bowl, combine the first 4 ingredients; press lightly into a greased 13 x 9-inch pan. Bake at 350° for 25-30 minutes or until golden brown, stirring every 10 minutes to form coarse crumbs. Cool. Divide crumb mixture in half; press half into the same baking pan. In a mixing bowl, beat pudding mixes and milk. Fold in whipped topping; spoon over the crust. Top with remaining crumb mixture. Cover and refrigerate overnight. Garnish with strawberries if desired. Serves 12-16.

Mrs. Norman (Marlena) Miller

Rhubarb Cream Dessert

2 c. crushed graham crackers
¼ c. sugar
½ c. butter
4 c. rhubarb

2 c. sugar
¾ c. + 2 T. strawberry gelatin
2 c. miniature marshmallows
1 c. whipped cream

Melt butter in pan; add crushed graham crackers and ¼ c. sugar. Press crumb mixture into 8 x 12-inch pan. Cook rhubarb slightly; add 2 c. sugar and gelatin. Cool to lukewarm. Add miniature marshmallows. Let stand to cool. When cool add whipped cream and pour into crumb-lined pan. Chill until firm.

Mrs. Joe (Susie) Delagrange

Strawberry Pretzel Dessert

Crust:
3 T. sugar
Cream Cheese Filling:
½ c. powdered sugar
1 8-oz. pkg. cream cheese
Strawberry Filling:
1 6-oz. pkg. strawberry Jell-O
2 c. hot water

2 c. crushed pretzels
¾ c. margarine, melted

2 c. miniature marshmallows
1 pkg. whipped topping

1 qt. frozen strawberries

Mix sugar, pretzels, and margarine and put into 9 x 13-inch pan. Bake 15 minutes at 350°. Mix powdered sugar, cream cheese, marshmallows, and whipped topping and put on top of baked pretzels. Strawberry filling: When slightly thickened spread on top of cream cheese layer. Chill.

Miriam Miller

Tapioca Pudding

2 qt. milk
⅔ c. pearl tapioca
3 eggs, beaten
2 c. sugar

2 heaping T. cornstarch
2 tsp. vanilla
¼ tsp. salt

Heat the milk and tapioca to boiling, stirring occasionally. Mix the rest of the ingredients together in a bowl. Add several cups of the hot milk, beating with beater; add to the rest of the hot milk. Heat to boiling. A dab of butter and marshmallows added makes it good. Cool slowly. If desired, you can add bananas to serve.

Mrs. Nathan (Mattie) Miller

Baby Pearl Tapioca

7 c. water
1½ c. tapioca
pinch salt
1 c. sugar

1 3-oz. box Jell-O
whipped cream
fruit

Bring water and salt to a boil. Slowly add tapioca. Cook 10-12 minutes. Stir occasionally. Take off stove and cover tightly for 5 minutes. Then add sugar and Jell-O. Cool. Add whipped cream and fruit.

Esther Miller

Yogurt

1 gal. skim milk	2 T. vanilla
2 T. plain gelatin	4 T. plain yogurt
½ c. cold water	1½ c. sugar

Heat milk in large kettle to 190°. While heating, soak gelatin in cold water. Add to milk once it reaches 190°, then cool to 130°. Add vanilla, yogurt, and sugar. Beat until smooth. Pour through wire strainer into 5-qt. ice-cream pail. Cover and put in warm place, such as in oven with only pilot on, for 5-8 hours. Chill. Add pie filling or preserves or peanut butter for variation. Thicken any fruit you add.

Mrs. Marcus (Mary) Gingerich
Mrs. Ernest (Mary Ellen) Miller

Apple Cheese Dessert

1½ to 2 qt. apple pie filling	1 T. vanilla
2 8-oz. pkg. cream cheese, softened	1 bag of caramels or
2 cans ready-made biscuits	1 jar Smucker's caramel
(Pillsbury Grands work best)	½ to ¾ c. sugar
1 c. chopped pecans	

Take apart each biscuit; flatten them along bottom and halfway up sides of a 13 x 9-inch pan. (Pillsbury Grands biscuits work best because they are a larger biscuit.) In medium bowl thoroughly mix softened cream cheese, vanilla, and sugar. Spread this mixture over crust. Spread apple pie filling over cream cheese mixture. Bake at 350° until sides of crust look golden. Remove from oven; drizzle hot caramel over top; sprinkle with pecans. Perfect dessert; takes hardly any effort. Always a favorite!

Mrs. Gregory (Denise) Rich

We'll get more from a sermon if we learn to listen like a Christian instead of a critic.

Lemon Pudding Dessert

1 c. cold butter or margarine
2 c. flour
1 8-oz. pkg. cream cheese, softened
1 c. powdered sugar

1 8-oz. container Cool Whip, divided
3 c. cold milk
2 3.4-oz. pkg. instant lemon
  pudding mix

In a bowl, cut butter into the flour until crumbly. Press into an ungreased 13 x 9-inch baking pan. Bake at 350° for 18-22 minutes or until set. Cool on a wire rack. In a mixing bowl, beat cream cheese and sugar until smooth. Fold in 1 c. whipped topping. Spread over crust. In a mixing bowl, beat milk and pudding mix on low speed for 2 minutes. Carefully spread over the cream cheese layer. Top with the remaining whipped topping. Refrigerate for at least 1 hour. Serves 12-16.

Mrs. Norman (Marlena) Miller

Raisin Delight

Batter:
¼ c. butter
2 c. flour
4 tsp. baking powder
Syrup:
1 c. brown sugar
1½ c. raisins

1 c. white sugar
1 c. milk

1 T. butter
2 tsp. vanilla
4 c. boiling water

Mix together batter ingredients and pour into greased pan. Boil syrup ingredients together for 5 minutes and pour on top of batter. Bake at 350° for 30-40 minutes or until done.

Mrs. Nathan (Mattie) Miller

Oreo Pudding

1 large pkg. Oreo cookies
1 large container Cool Whip

½ gal. vanilla ice cream, softened

Crush the cookies; put some in the bottom of 9 x 13-inch pan. Mix rest of crumbs with other ingredients, then pour mixture in pan and freeze.

Ruth Maria Herschberger

Ice-Cream Dessert

½ c. graham cracker crumbs
3 T. melted butter
1½ c. Oreo cookie crumbs
1 pkg. vanilla pudding mix
1 pkg. butter pecan pudding mix

2 c. milk
1 qt. vanilla ice cream
Cool Whip
3 Butterfinger candy bars

Mix first 3 ingredients and pat into 9 x 13-inch pan to make a crumb crust. Mix together pudding mixes, milk, and ice cream. Pour over crust and cover with Cool Whip. Crush Butterfinger bars and put on top.

Mrs. Perry (Delores) Herschberger

Ice-Cream Dessert (Frozen)

3 bananas
nuts
  Crust:
1½ c. graham cracker crumbs
½ c. margarine, melted
  Sauce:
1 c. chocolate chips
2 c. powdered sugar

1 qt. ice cream

¼ c. sugar

½ c. margarine
1 tsp. vanilla
1½ c. evaporated milk

Crust: Combine crumbs, margarine, and sugar and press into 13 x 9-inch pan. Slice 3 bananas over crust. Put about 1 quart ice cream over bananas. Sprinkle nuts over ice cream and freeze. Sauce: Melt margarine and chocolate chips; add powdered sugar and milk. Cook until thick, about 30 minutes on low heat. Add vanilla and cool. Pour over ice cream and freeze. Top with whipped cream and nuts and freeze.

Esther Miller

Almond Delight

12 oz. chocolate chips
⅔ c. peanut butter
1 gal. vanilla ice cream

6 c. Almond Delight cereal
  (or Frosted Flakes)

Melt chocolate chips and peanut butter over low heat; stir in cereal and cool. Reserve 1 c. coated cereal for topping. Mix the rest of the coated cereal with the ice cream. Pour into a 9 x 13-inch pan. Freeze and enjoy!

Mrs. Jonas (Elizabeth) Wagler

The Authentic Amish Cookbook

Raspberry Swirl

¾ c. graham cracker crumbs
3 T. melted butter or margarine
2 T. sugar
3 eggs, separated
1 8-oz. pkg. cream cheese

1 c. sugar
⅛ tsp. salt
1 c. heavy cream, whipped
1 10-oz. pkg. frozen raspberries,
  partially thawed

Combine crumbs, butter, and 2 T. sugar. Press into pan. Beat egg yolks until thick. Add cream cheese, 1 c. sugar, and salt. Beat until smooth and light. Beat egg whites until stiff peaks form. Fold egg whites and whipped cream into cheese mixture. Puree raspberries in a blender. Gently swirl half of puree through cheese filling; spread mixture in crust. Spoon remaining puree over top. Swirl with a knife. Freeze.

Kathryn Mary Kauffman

Quick and Easy Homemade Ice Cream

¾ qt. evaporated milk
2 pkg. vanilla instant pudding
2 c. white sugar

5 eggs
1 T. vanilla flavoring

Beat eggs and evaporated milk; put in instant pudding and mix well. Add rest of ingredients. Mix together and put in ice-cream freezer. Add milk until full line. Freeze and enjoy.

Mrs. Steve (Edith) Engbretson

Easy No-Cook Ice Cream

4 eggs, beaten until fluffy
¼ tsp. salt
4 c. milk
3 tsp. vanilla

¾ c. sugar
1 box instant vanilla pudding
4 c. or 1 32-oz. can Rich's or other
  nondairy topping, whipped

Mix all together and pour into 6-qt. freezer. Delicious! Variation: Bits of candy bar may be added just prior to freezing.

Mrs. Wilbur (Joann) Hochstetler
Mrs. John (Carolyn) Otto

Dairy Queen Ice Cream

3 T. Knox gelatin
1 c. cold water
7 c. milk
3 c. white sugar

1 tsp. salt
3 tsp. vanilla
4½ c. cream (can substitute
  with milk)

Soak gelatin in water. Heat milk to hot, but not to boiling. Remove from heat and add sugar, salt, and vanilla. Cool and add cream. Chill before freezing. Makes 1½ gallons.

Mrs. Kenneth (Martha) Miller

Cooked Ice Cream

1 gal. rich milk
3½ c. sugar
⅔ c. cornstarch

4 eggs
3 T. vanilla

Bring milk to boil in 8-qt. kettle. Add mixture of sugar, cornstarch, and eggs, which have been stirred until smooth. Bring all to a boil, stirring constantly. Remove from heat and add vanilla or preferred flavoring. Chill, then freeze. Will fill 6-qt. freezer.

Mrs. Earl (Irma) Chupp

Sherbet

2 c. water
1 c. sugar

1 c. Jell-O (any flavor)
2 qt. milk

Boil sugar and water together and add Jell-O. Chill until partly set, then add milk and freeze in ice-cream freezer.

Mrs. Edna Slabaugh

A wise man lays a firm foundation with the bricks that others throw at him.

Baked Custard

5 c. milk, scalded
10 eggs, well beaten
1½ c. sugar
1 tsp. vanilla

2 T. unflavored gelatin
½ c. milk
1 tsp. salt

Soak gelatin in ½ c. milk. Add all the other ingredients; mix well. Pour mixture into little Pyrex custard cups. Place cups into cake pans with 2 inches water. Bake at 400° for 10 minutes. Reduce to 350° and bake 45 minutes. Makes 10 1-c. servings.

Mrs. Omer (Martha) Miller

Cinnamon Pudding

Step 1:
2 c. brown sugar
1½ c. cold water

2 T. butter

Step 2:
1 c. sugar
2 T. butter
1 c. milk

2 scant c. flour
2 tsp. baking powder
2 tsp. cinnamon

Mix ingredients in step 1 and bring to a boil. Put step 2 mixture in bottom of 9 x 13-inch pan, then step 1 mixture, and sprinkle nuts on top (if desired). Bake 45 minutes at 350°. Serve with whipped cream. Also good with ice cream.

Mrs. John (Carolyn) Otto

Rhubarb Crunch

1¼ c. flour
1¼ c. oatmeal
1 c. brown sugar
½ c. melted butter
1 tsp. cinnamon

3 c. diced rhubarb
1 c. sugar
1 c. water
2 T. cornstarch
1 tsp. vanilla

Mix flour, oatmeal, brown sugar, melted butter, and cinnamon until crumbly. Press ½ of the crumbs into a 9 x 9-inch pan. Put rhubarb on top. Mix sugar, water, cornstarch, and vanilla; heat to boiling, stirring well. Pour over rhubarb. Top with remaining crumbs. Bake at 350° for approximately an hour.

Mrs. Jonas (Elizabeth) Wagler

Rhubarb Crunch

Crumb Topping:

1 c. flour	1 tsp. cinnamon
1 tsp. baking powder	¾ c. firmly packed brown sugar
1 tsp. salt	½ c. melted butter

Fruit Mixture:

4 c. (more or less) diced rhubarb	2 rounded T. Perma-flo
1 c. sugar	1 c. water
pinch salt	½ c. strawberry Jell-O

Mix crumb topping until crumbly. Press ½ in a greased 9-inch layer pan. Cover with rhubarb. In saucepan bring water to boiling. Mix Perma-flo, sugar, salt, Jell-O, and enough cold water to make a paste. Stir into boiling water; cook and remove from heat. Pour over rhubarb. Cover with remaining crumbs. Bake 1 hour at 350°. Serve hot or cold. Note: Cook the Perma-flo syrup and cool completely before using. This will prevent the bottom crust from becoming so hard. (I have learned.) Serves 8.

Lena Yoder

Feathery Light Dessert Dumplings

1 c. sifted pastry flour	2 T. butter
1½ tsp. baking powder	⅓ c. milk
½ tsp. salt	1 egg, beaten
3 T. sugar	1 tsp. vanilla

Sift dry ingredients together in bowl; cut in butter with pastry blender until mixture is crumbly. Pour in milk and vanilla; add egg. Mix only until flour is dampened (dough should be lumpy). Drop by spoonful onto simmering fruit, cooked this way: Drain 5 c. sliced, canned peaches, berries, or other fruits. Put in shallow kettle with 1 c. of the juice. Cover and simmer 3 minutes over direct heat before adding dumplings. Cover dumplings tightly and steam 12 minutes without removing cover. Makes 6 fluffy dumplings. Serves 6.

Lena Yoder

Swallow your pride
occasionally.
It's not fattening.
Frank Tyger

Snowball Peaches

8 oz. softened cream cheese
2 T. chopped dates
1 c. pineapple tidbits, drained

15 canned peach halves
fresh mint leaves, optional

In a mixing bowl, mix first 3 ingredients until blended. Place drained peach halves on a serving platter. Fill with cream cheese mixture and garnish with mint if desired. Serves 15.

Mrs. Omer (Martha) Miller

Apple Danish

Pastry:
3 c. all-purpose flour
½ tsp. salt
1 c. shortening

1 egg yolk
½ c. milk

Filling:
6 c. peeled, sliced apples
1½ c. sugar

¼ c. butter or margarine, melted
2 T. flour
1 tsp. ground cinnamon

Glaze:
1 egg white, lightly beaten
2 to 3 tsp. water

½ c. powdered sugar

In mixing bowl, combine flour and salt. Cut in shortening until mixture resembles coarse crumbs. Combine egg yolk and milk; add to flour mixture. Stir just until dough clings together. Divide dough in half. On lightly floured surface, roll ½ of dough into a 15 x 10-inch rectangle. Transfer to a greased pan; set aside. Toss together filling ingredients and spoon over pastry in pan. Roll out rest of dough into another 15 x 10-inch rectangle. Place over filling. Brush with the egg white. Bake at 375° for 40 minutes or until golden. Cool on rack. Combine powdered sugar and enough water to achieve a drizzling consistency. Drizzle over warm pastry. Cut into squares. Serve warm or cold. Serves 20-24.

Mrs. Nathan (Mattie) Miller

A smile is a crooked line that sets a lot of things straight.

Baked Apples

8-10 peeled, quartered apples
1 T. butter
½ c. brown sugar

3 T. Perma-flo
2 c. water

Place apples in greased 2-qt. baking dish. Dot with butter; mix rest of ingredients. Pour over apples. Cover; bake at 350° 45 minutes to 1 hour. Serve warm or chilled with whipped cream.

Mrs. Omer (Martha) Miller

If we rise above the storm clouds we will see the sunshine!

. . .

There is a song in the night
For those who walk in the light.

. . .

Remember—there's blue sky behind the blackest cloud.

Charlotte Maria Tucker

Miscellaneous Recipes

Just As I Am

Behold the Lamb of God. —John 1:29

Charlotte Elliot, 1789-1871

William B. Bradbury, 1816-1868

1. Just as I am, with-out one plea, But that Thy blood was shed for me, And
2. Just as I am, and wait-ing not To rid my soul of one dark blot, To
3. Just as I am, though tossed about With many a con-flict, many a doubt, Fight-
4. Just as I am, poor, wretched, blind; Sight, rich-es, heal-ing of the mind, Yea,
5. Just as I am, Thou wilt re-ceive, Wilt welcome, pardon, cleanse, relieve; Be-

that Thou bidd'st me come to Thee, O Lamb of God, I come! I come!
Thee whose blood can cleanse each spot, O Lamb of God, I come! I come!
ings and fears with-in, with-out, O Lamb of God, I come! I come!
all I need, in Thee I find, O Lamb of God, I come! I come!
cause Thy prom-ise I be - lieve, O Lamb of God, I come! I come! A-MEN.

Venison or Beef Jerky

5 to 7 lb. venison or beef
1 c. soy sauce
4 tsp. onion powder
1 tsp. Tender Quick
2 tsp. black pepper

2½ T. brown sugar
½ c. liquid smoke
2½ tsp. garlic powder
2 tsp. salt
1 tsp. cayenne pepper

Slice meat in ¼-inch slices (will slice easily if meat is frozen) or cut in 1-inch chunks. Mix all other ingredients together and put in glass bowl. Marinate 12 hours in spices in fridge. Drain and save juice for next batch. Place meat in single layers on cookie sheets. Put in 150° oven. Jerky is done in 8 hours. Turn at 4 hours. Let set 2 hours to dry. If oven is set higher than 150° it may not take quite 8 hours.

Mrs. Roy (Martha) Hershberger

Pickled Heart

½ c. sugar
1 c. vinegar
½ tsp. salt

¼ c. water
1 pt. chunked heart or tongue meat

Cut meat in small chunks. Boil in water until soft. Drain. (Cooking water may be used for the water in this recipe.) Mix brine ingredients and pour onto meat. Makes quart jar ⅔ full. Store in refrigerator.

Mrs. Jerry (Ruth) Gingerich

Easy Homemade Noodles

white flour
egg yolks from 4 dozen eggs
 (should be at least 3 c.)

1½ c. boiling water
½ tsp. salt (optional)

Put enough flour in a Tupperware Fix N Mix bowl to weigh 4 pounds, including bowl. Beat egg yolks with salt and water until foamy. Make sure water is boiling hot, then beat quickly. The longer you beat the yolks and water, the lighter they will be in color. So if you want yellow noodles, do not overbeat. Now pour this mixture into flour and stir with a large spoon until stiff. Shape into balls with hands. Put the lid on and let stand for 10 minutes. Then knead a bit and it's ready to put through noodle cutter. Use rolling pin to roll out and cut in strips. (This dough is not so sticky to handle.)

Mrs. James (Rosanna) Miller

Grilled Ham and Egg Salad Sandwich

6 hard-boiled eggs, chopped
1 c. diced, fully cooked ham
½ c. finely chopped celery
1 T. minced onion
½ c. mayonnaise
  Batter:
½ c. cornmeal
½ c. all-purpose flour
1 tsp. baking powder

2 tsp. prepared mustard
½ tsp. salt
¼ tsp. pepper
12 slices whole wheat or white bread
cooking oil

1 tsp. salt
2 c. milk
2 eggs, lightly beaten

Mix first 8 ingredients; spread on 6 slices of bread. Top with remaining bread and set aside. In a bowl, whisk batter ingredients until well blended. Heat about ½ inch oil in a deep skillet. Dip sandwiches into batter. Fry in hot oil for 3 minutes on each side or until golden brown. Drain on paper towels. Serves 6.

Kathryn Mary Kauffman

Muenster Cheese

2½ gal. skimmed milk
1 T. baking soda
½ c. butter

1 to 2 c. sour cream
1 T. salt

Let milk sour in a large kettle until thick and set. Then scald until hot enough that it is uncomfortable for the hand. Pour into cheesecloth or any lightweight cloth. Let hang until curds are dry, overnight or about 12 hours. (You can squeeze them dry if you want to finish the same day.) Now crumble curds (a Salsa Master chops them up nicely) and mix 1 T. soda and ½ c. butter into them. Let set for 2 hours, then put in double boiler. Add 1 c. sour cream and melt. When melted, add rest of sour cream and 1 T. salt. Mix well and pour into buttered mold. Completely chill and slice. This is a basic recipe, very adjustable; use more or less cream to suit your taste. Sweet cream works too.

Mrs. Marcus (Mary) Gingerich

I do not go alone through the hours of this day, for Thou art with me.

Cheese Spread

3 2-lb. boxes cheese (like Velveeta)   5½ c. milk (or a little more),
1 stick margarine   scalded

Add cheese and margarine to scalded milk. Heat until melted.

Mrs. Glen (Marilyn) Miller

Griddle Cakes

2 c. flour   2 eggs, beaten
5 tsp. baking powder   2 c. milk
2 tsp. salt   6 T. melted shortening
3 T. sugar

Sift together flour, baking powder, salt, and sugar. Beat eggs in mixing bowl. Add milk, shortening, and flour mixture; stir until blended. Heat griddle pan. (Sprinkle a few drops of water on it. When drops stay round and bounce about, the temperature is right.) Grease lightly. Pour about ¼ c. for each griddle cake. Bake until top side is full of bubbles that begin to break and edges are dry. Turn; brown on other side. Makes 2 dozen.

Lena Yoder

Oatmeal Pancakes

1½ c. quick oats   1 tsp. sugar
2 c. buttermilk*   1 tsp. soda
2 beaten eggs   1 tsp. salt
½ c. wheat flour   chunk of butter or shortening

*If milk is used instead of buttermilk, add 1 tsp. vinegar per cup of milk. Also add a little more flour.

This batter is a little thin and runny. Spread peanut butter on pancakes with syrup on top. Serves 4.

Mrs. Ernest (Mary Ellen) Miller

When you speak always remember that God is one of your hearers.

Amish Proverb

Sunrise Pancakes

1 c. all-purpose flour	2 eggs, slightly beaten
2 T. sugar	½ c. plain yogurt
½ tsp. baking soda	½ c. water
1 tsp. baking powder	2 T. butter or margarine, melted
½ tsp. salt	
Vanilla Cream Syrup:	
½ c. sugar	1 tsp. vanilla
½ c. light corn syrup	1 nectarine, diced (optional)
½ c. whipping cream	

Prepare syrup by combining sugar, corn syrup, and cream in a 1-qt. saucepan. Cook, stirring constantly, over medium heat until sugar is dissolved. Simmer 2 minutes or until syrup thickens slightly. Remove from heat. Stir in vanilla and nectarine. Makes 1 cup.

For pancakes, combine flour, sugar, baking powder, baking soda, and salt in large bowl. Combine eggs, yogurt, and water in medium bowl. Whisk in butter. Pour liquid ingredients into dry ingredients; stir until moistened. Pour about ¼ c. batter onto a hot griddle for each pancake and spread batter out to make 5-inch circles. Makes about 8 pancakes.

Doris Yoder

Waffles

2 c. sifted flour	1½ c. milk
¾ tsp. salt	2 eggs, well-beaten
2½ tsp. baking powder	5 T. canola oil

Sift flour, measure, add baking powder and salt; mix. Add eggs and milk, then oil. Mix only until smooth. Bake in hot waffle iron 2-3 minutes.

Mrs. Omer (Martha) Miller

Pancake Syrup

2½ c. brown sugar	1 tsp. butter flavoring
⅔ c. light corn syrup	1½ tsp. maple flavoring
1½ c. white sugar	1 tsp. vanilla

Bring above ingredients, except vanilla, to a boil with 2 c. water, stirring often. Simmer 5 minutes. Remove from heat and add vanilla. Keeps well in refrigerator.

Mrs. John (Carolyn) Otto

Marshmallow Creme

2 c. white sugar
1 c. water
2½ c. light corn syrup

½ c. light corn syrup, warmed
1 c. egg whites
1 tsp. vanilla

Cook first 3 ingredients to soft ball stage (250°). Cool 5 minutes. While cooling, place warmed corn syrup in mixing bowl. Add egg whites. Beat slowly until mixed, then beat hard until fluffy. Gradually add first mixture in fine stream, beating all the time. Add vanilla. Beat very hard for 3 minutes. Store in jar. Don't cover until cool.

To make flavored marshmallow creme to use as jam: Mix 3 oz. strawberry Jell-O into the hot syrup before adding to beaten egg whites.

Mrs. Perry (Delores) Herschberger

Dandelion Jelly

1 qt. dandelion blossoms
1 pkg. pectin
4½ c. sugar

1 qt. water
1 tsp. lemon or orange extract

In the morning, pick dandelions without any stems attached. Boil blossoms in water for 3 minutes. Drain off 3 c. liquid. Add pectin, extract, and sugar. Boil about 3 minutes. Seal in jars. Its taste resembles honey.

Mary Ann Mast

Honey Butter

1 c. butter
½ c. honey

2 tsp. cinnamon

Heat butter and honey until melted. Stir until dissolved and melted. Add cinnamon. Delicious on warm bread fresh out of the oven!

Mrs. Orlie (Mary) Troyer

No matter how much we have failed, the love of God never ceases.

Play Dough

2 c. flour
3 T. vegetable oil
4 tsp. cream of tartar

2 c. water
1 c. salt
food color

Mix all these ingredients together in a pan. Cook over medium heat until mixture starts boiling or forms a ball (about 2-3 minutes). Remove from heat and cool enough to handle. Knead dough like bread until smooth and supple.

Rachel Troyer

Play Dough

2½ c. flour
½ c. salt
3 T. cooking oil

1 T. alum
2 c. boiling water
food coloring

Add coloring to water before mixing all other ingredients thoroughly.

Mrs. Glen (Marilyn) Miller

Finger Paint

⅓ c. cornstarch
3 T. sugar

2 c. cold water
food coloring

Mix cornstarch, sugar, and water in 1-qt. saucepan. Cook and stir over medium heat about 5 minutes or until thickened; remove from heat. Divide the mixture into separate cups or containers. Tint mixture in each container with a different food color. Stir several times until cool. Store in an airtight container. This paint works best if you use it the same day you make it.

Mrs. Ben (Keturah) Troyer

Before you flare up at anyone's faults, take time to count ten— ten of your own.

Large Quantity Recipes

Tell Me the Story of Jesus

Go and shew John again those things which ye do hear and see. —Matthew 11:4

Fanny J. Crosby, 1820-1915   John R. Sweney, 1837-1899

1. Tell me the sto - ry of Je - sus, Write on my heart ev - 'ry word;
2. Fast - ing a - lone in the des - ert, Tell of the days that are past,
3. Tell of the cross where they nailed Him, Writh - ing in an - guish and pain;

REF. — *Tell me the sto - ry of Je - sus, Write on my heart ev - 'ry word;*

FINE

Tell me the sto - ry most pre - cious, Sweet - est that ev - er was heard.
How for our sins He was tempt - ed, Yet was tri - um-phant at last.
Tell of the grave where they laid Him, Tell how He liv - eth a - gain.

Tell me the sto - ry most pre - cious, Sweet - est that ev - er was heard.

Tell how the an - gels, in cho - rus, Sang as they wel-comed His birth,
Tell of the years of His la - bor, Tell of the sor - row He bore,
Love in that sto - ry so ten - der, Clear - er than ev - er I see:

D. C. for Refrain

"Glo - ry to God in the high - est! Peace and good ti - dings to earth."
He was de-spised and af - flict - ed, Home-less, re - ject - ed and poor.
Stay, let me weep while you whis - per, Love paid the ran-som for me.

Mom's Pie Dough

1 lb. or 2 c. lard
5 c. pastry flour
½ tsp. salt

1 c. liquid (1 egg, 1 T. vinegar,
water)

Blend lard, flour, and salt. In 1 cup measure, mix beaten egg and vinegar and fill cup with water. Mix crumbs and liquid. Makes approximately 8 single crusts.

Mrs. Loyal (Dorcas) Gingerich

Mixed Fruit

6 gal. pineapple chunks, drained
4 gal. sliced peaches, drained
4 gal. diced peaches, drained

2 gal. red grapes, cut in half
2 gal. green grapes, cut in half

Drain pineapple and peaches well. Divide juice in 2 8-qt. kettles. Take 2 c. sugar and 3½ c. Perma-flo. Mix and add to juice in each kettle. Cook until thick. If too thick, add extra pineapple juice. When chilled pour over fruit and mix. Serves 450.

Mrs. Omer (Martha) Miller

Scrambled Eggs

10 dozen eggs, beaten
2½ T. salt
2½ qt. hot milk

1 c. melted butter
3 lb. cut and fried bacon
2 lb. grated Colby cheese

Chop and fry bacon. Add salt and milk to eggs. Divide melted butter in 3 Pyrex 13 x 9 x 2-inch pans. Then divide egg mixture into pans; divide and sprinkle bacon over tops; sprinkle with cheese. Bake at 350° for 45-50 minutes. Serves 100.

Mrs. Omer (Martha) Miller

Nobody cares how much you know, until they know how much you care.

Theodore Roosevelt

Chicken Dressing

3 loaves bread, cubed and toasted
2 c. shredded carrots
12 eggs, beaten
2 qt. milk
2 qt. potato water
3 T. salt
3 qt. cubed potatoes
2 qt. chicken broth with meat

2 c. chopped onion
1 qt. diced celery
¾ T. Accent seasoning
¾ T. pepper
¾ T. seasoned salt
3 T. chicken soup base
2 sticks butter

Combine first 10 ingredients in 13-qt. mixing bowl. Melt 2 sticks butter in sauce-pan. Add Accent, pepper, seasoned salt, and chicken soup base. Mix well; pour in large, buttered baking dish. Cover with foil. Bake at 350° for 2 hours. Serves 75.

Mrs. Omer (Martha) Miller

Mashed Potatoes

1 8-qt. kettle potatoes
4 8-oz. pkg. cream cheese
2½ c. sour cream

3 T. salt or to taste
whipping cream

Cook potatoes until very soft. Add 3 T. lemon juice to water while cooking. Drain and mash. Beat in sour cream and cream cheese until fluffy; add salt and whipping cream to desired consistency. If using at once, put in baking dish and bake at 350° for 30 minutes. These may be made ahead and frozen until ready to use. (Stir several times while heating.) Takes 14 8-qt. kettles for 500 people.

Mrs. Jerome (Rose) Graber

Pie Dough

3 lb. shortening (all-purpose)
5⅛ lb. pastry flour (17½ c.)

¾ T. baking powder
3 c. cold water

Mix first 3 ingredients. Add water and mix. Roll out into pie pans. Freeze some for later use. Makes approximately 25 single crusts.

Mrs. Ernest (Mary Ellen) Miller

Do good with what you have or it will do you no good.

William Penn

Poor Man's Steak

50 lb. hamburger
4 qt. cracker crumbs
4 c. milk
Sauce for meat:
17 cans cream of mushroom soup
20 soup cans water

5 T. + 1 tsp. salt
3 T. pepper
2½ qt. onions

6 cans cream of chicken soup

Mix all ingredients except for the sauce and press into cookie sheets. Refrigerate overnight and then cut into pieces. Mix sauce with wire whip. You may either grill the meat or roll in flour and fry until brown, then layer in roasters, putting a layer of sauce over each layer of meat. Takes approximately 3 batches to serve 500 people.

Mrs. Jerome (Rose) Graber

Pie Crumbs

10 c. oatmeal
10 c. brown sugar
11 c. flour
4 tsp. baking powder

5 c. margarine
1 T. baking soda
1 tsp. salt

This can also be used for crunch and can be frozen until ready to use. Yields approximately 30 cups.

Mrs. Ernest (Mary Ellen) Miller

Peanut Butter for Church

10 c. brown sugar
5 c. water
¾ c. light corn syrup

3 qt. marshmallow creme
5 to 6 lb. peanut butter

Boil first 3 ingredients 10-15 minutes. Cool off. Add marshmallow creme and peanut butter and stir together.

Mrs. Edna Slabaugh

If your troubles are deep-seated and long-standing, try kneeling.

Inspirational Gems for Mothers

The Bible is full of messages: One which especially pertains to mothers is found in Titus chapter 2. It is where the older women are instructed to teach the younger women to be sober, to love their husbands, to love their children, to be discreet, chaste, keepers at home, good, obedient to their own husbands, that the word of God be not blasphemed.

SOBER is marked by an earnest, thoughtful character, unhurried, calm, moderate, and serious.

LOVE is an affection based on admiration and common interest, unselfish loyalty.

DISCREET means having or showing good judgment in conduct and speech; being modest. The dictionary refers to discretion as the warmth and elegance of a civilized home.

CHASTE means pure in thought and act, having control of one's impulses and actions.

A KEEPER AT HOME is one who keeps—one fit or suitable to be a keeper, a protector, profitable, pleasant, wholesome, well-founded.

Thinking that you aren't as good as someone else or that you can never do anything right is as wrong as thinking you are better than others and can do everything right.

The mother plays a vital role in the general atmosphere of the home... God has blessed her with a house she can call her castle, her own family (a gift from the Lord), strength to work and care for her most precious family.

Make your home a haven of rest for your family. Expect and enforce prompt obedience.

Saturday night work should end in proper time—being spiritually prepared for Sunday is more important than material gain.

Be on time with meals as much as possible. It has a big value in being orderly.

Organizing will simplify your life. The old saying "A place for everything and everything in its place" is good advice.

It is much easier to pick up the toys, straighten up the house, and wash dishes before we retire, than to face those neglected tasks, plus doing our regular work, in the morning.

Health Food Recipes

Appetizers and Beverages

Komm zu dem Heiland

George F. Root, 1820-1895
Übers Ernst H. Gebhardt, 1832-1899

George F. Root, 1820-1895

1. Komm zu dem Hei - land, kom - me noch heut! Folg Sei-nem Wort, jetzt
2. Komm, o mein Kind, und hö - re Sein Wort! Gib Ihm dein Herz, und
3. Glau - be nur fest, der Herr nimmt dich an! O fühlst du Ihn nicht

ist es noch Zeit! Er ist uns nah, zum Seg - nen be - reit,
folg Ihm so - fort! Er ist ein sich - rer, e - wi - ger Hort;
jetzt dir schon nahn? Mit Lieb' und Gnad' will Er dich um-fahn,

REFRAIN

Und ruft so freund-lich: „Komm!" Herr - lich, herr - lich wird es ein-mal sein,
Drum mach dich auf und komm!
Komm nur, o Sün - der, komm!

Wenn wir ziehn, von Sün- de frei und rein, In das ge - lob - te

Ka - na - an ein! Je - sus, sieh her, ich komm!

Amish Chai

¼ c. carob powder
½ tsp. cinnamon
¼ tsp. ginger
¼ c. honey

3 T. water
½ tsp. vanilla
¼ tsp. maple flavoring
1 qt. milk

Thoroughly mix first 4 ingredients; add water. Heat over medium-low heat, stirring constantly, until bubbly. Add 1 qt. milk and heat to scalding, then add flavorings. Stir well, then allow to settle a few minutes before dipping out into cups. Serves 4.

Mrs. Elvie (Rebekah) Miller

Eggnog

1 egg, beaten
¾ c. milk
½ banana, mashed
½ tsp. cinnamon

¼ tsp. nutmeg, optional
honey to taste
½ tsp. vanilla

Beat the egg first; add all other ingredients and beat thoroughly. This seems to be a real energizer, especially after being sick. Also good to drink when ill.

Mrs. Monroe (Elsie) Miller

Fruit Slush

½ c. raw sugar
3 c. boiling water
6 oz. frozen orange juice

20-oz. unsweetened crushed
   pineapple with juice
3 sliced bananas

Mix sugar and water until sugar is dissolved, then cool. Mix orange juice with 1 can water. Add rest of ingredients. Freeze. Allow to thaw until slushy before serving.

Mrs. Omer (Martha) Miller

Beware of the man who knows the answer before he understands the question.

Garden Tea Concentrate

4 qt. water   sweetener, if desired
4 c. fresh tea leaves

Bring 4 qt. water to a boil. Remove from heat and add 4 c. fresh tea leaves. Cover and let set for 20 minutes. Remove leaves. Sweetener may be added if you wish. Cool and freeze. To serve, mix one part concentrate and two parts water, or to suit your taste.

Mrs. Dewayne (Edna Sue) Miller

Almond Milk

½ c. raw almonds   2 c. water
1 T. maple syrup

Option: Blanch almonds by placing them in 1 c. boiling water. Let stand a little, then pop off skins. This makes a whiter milk. We love it without blanching too.

Place almonds in blender and grind to a fine powder. Add sweetener and 1 c. water. Blend for 1 or 2 minutes to form a smooth cream. With blender running on high, add remaining cup of water slowly through opening of blender lid. Blend 2 minutes. Place a fine strainer (medium size) over large bowl. I like to set it on my glass measuring pitcher. To ensure a smooth milk, line the strainer with cheesecloth. Pour almond milk slowly into strainer and allow to filter through, stirring with spoon to speed up the straining process. Once the milk is strained, bring the sides of the cheesecloth together and slowly but firmly squeeze out the remaining milk from the fiber. Store in a glass jar in the refrigerator. Almond milk will keep 4 to 5 days. Yield: 1 pint milk.

Mrs. John (Rosanna) Bowman

Blunt remarks, like dull knives, often inflict the severest wounds.

Soups and Salads

Sweet By and By

I go to prepare a place for you. —John 14:2

Sanford F. Bennett, 1836-1898   Joseph P. Webster, 1819-1875

1. There's a land that is fair - er than day, And by faith we can
2. We shall sing on that beau - ti - ful shore The me - lo - di - ous
3. To our boun - ti - ful Fa - ther a - bove, We will of - fer the

see it a - far; For the Fa - ther waits o - ver the way, To pre-
songs of the blest, And our spir - its shall sor - row no more, Not a
trib - ute of praise For the glo - ri - ous gift of His love, And the

REFRAIN

pare us a dwell-ing-place there. In the sweet   by and
sigh for the bless-ing of rest.
bless-ings that hal - low our days.   In the sweet

by,   We shall meet on that beau - ti - ful shore;   In the
    by and by,   by and by;

sweet   by and by,   We shall meet on that beau - ti - ful shore.
    In the sweet   by and by,

Dilly Beans

2 lb. small tender green beans
1 tsp. red pepper
4 cloves garlic
4 large heads dill

2 c. water
2 c. white vinegar
¼ c. pickling salt

Pack green beans in pint jars. To each jar add ¼ tsp. pepper, 1 clove garlic, and 1 head dill. Heat water, salt, and vinegar; bring to boil. Pour over beans. Seal. Makes 4 pints.

Mrs. David (Rhoda) Miller

Chili Soup

2 qt. tomato juice
1½ qt. water
½ c. brown sugar
2 T. chili powder

onion salt to taste
medium or large onion
1 lb. hamburger
1 c. lentils

Cut up onion and fry with hamburger. Put juice, water, brown sugar, and chili powder in 4-qt. kettle. Add fried hamburger with onions. Bring to boil; add lentils and onion salt. Simmer slowly for 1 hour or more, stirring occasionally. Can use more juice and less water or vice versa according to how rich you want it to be. Makes 4 qt.

Mrs. Monroe (Elsie) Miller

Lentil Soup

½ c. butter
1 onion, chopped
1 c. chopped celery
2 c. carrots
2 tsp. salt
¼ tsp. pepper

1 qt. chunked tomatoes
8 c. water
1 c. lentils
¾ c. brown rice
5 to 6 bay leaves
1 T. rosemary

Sauté onions and celery in the butter in 8-qt. kettle until lightly brown. Add rest of ingredients. Cook over medium heat for 45 minutes or until rice is done. Serves 8.

Mrs. John (Loma) Kauffman

Hearty Chicken Stew

1 c. cubed, cooked chicken	½ c. lentils
4 c. chicken broth and/or water	1 tsp. salt
½ c. diced celery	dash pepper
½ c. diced carrots	dried parsley to taste and
¼ c. chopped onion	other seasonings you prefer
½ c. pearl barley	

Simmer barley and lentils with chicken and broth for approximately 1 hour. Add vegetables and seasonings; simmer ½ hour more. Add more liquid if needed. Season to your family's taste. I also use chicken seasoning and vegetable flakes.

Mrs. Stephen (Amelia) Miller

Hearty Hamburger Soup

2 T. butter	2 c. tomato juice
1 lb. ground beef	1 tsp. seasoning salt
1 c. sliced carrots	4 c. milk
½ c. chopped onions	½ tsp. pepper
½ c. sliced celery	1½ tsp. salt
1 c. diced potatoes	½ c. flour

Melt butter, add meat and onions. Fry. Stir in remaining ingredients except flour and milk. Cover and let cook over low heat about 20-25 minutes. Combine flour with 1 c. milk. Stir into soup mixture and boil. Add remaining milk and stir frequently. Do not boil after adding the remaining milk.

Mrs. Dewayne (Edna Sue) Miller

Experience is the name everyone gives to their mistakes.

Oscar Wilde

Apple Cabbage Slaw

6 c. shredded cabbage
3 medium red apples, chopped
1 5-oz. can evaporated milk

¼ c. lemon juice
2 T. raw sugar
2 tsp. grated onion

In a large bowl, toss the cabbage and apples. In a small bowl, combine the remaining ingredients. Pour over cabbage mixture and toss to coat. Refrigerate until serving. Serves 10.

Mrs. Omer (Martha) Miller

Hearty Chili Soup

4 lb. hamburger
2 qt. cooked kidney beans
1 large onion

4 tsp. seasoned salt
2 tsp. chili powder
3 qt. tomato juice

Brown hamburger in skillet. Chop onion and add to hamburger. Add seasonings and kidney beans. Mix well and add tomato juice. Simmer for 30 minutes. This recipe may be made in large amounts for canning.

Mrs. Freeman (Wilma) Troyer

A bad habit is like a comfortable bed; easy to get into, but hard to get out of.

. . .

The teeth may be false, but let the tongue be true.

Notes

Breads, Rolls, and Cereals

How Beautiful Heaven Must Be

Revelation 21:1-27

A.S. Bridgewater, 20th Century

A.P. Bland, 20th Century

1. We read of a place that's called heav-en, It's made for the pure and the free;
2. In heav-en, no drooping nor pin - ing, No wish-ing for else-where to be;
3. Pure wa-ters of life there are flow - ing, And all who will drink may be free;
4. The an-gels so sweet-ly are sing - ing, Up there by the beau-ti - ful sea;

These truths in God's Word He has giv - en, How beau-ti-ful heav-en must be.
God's light is for - ev - er there shin-ing, How beau-ti-ful heav-en must be.
Rare jew - els of splen-dor are glow-ing, How beau-ti-ful heav-en must be.
Sweet chords from their gold harps are ring-ing, How beau-ti-ful heav-en must be.

REFRAIN

How beau-ti - ful heav-en must be,...... Sweet home of the hap - py and free;
must be,

Fair ha - ven of rest for the wea - ry, How beau - ti-ful heav-en must be.

100% Whole Wheat Bread

2 eggs	2 heaping T. wheat gluten
4¼ c. water	3 T. yeast (heaping)
¾ c. oil	1 T. lecithin (heaping)
1½ T. salt	11½ c. wheat flour (organic)
¾ c. honey	

Knead until well mixed. Don't make too stiff. Let rise in warm place 1 hour. Put in pans and let rise until 1 inch above pans. Bake at 350° for 35 minutes. Yields 6-7 loaves.

Mrs. Glen (Marilyn) Miller

100% Whole Wheat Bread

4 c. lukewarm water	2 T. salt
2 eggs	½ c. vegetable oil
2 T. instant yeast	¼ c. honey
12 to 13 c. whole wheat flour, more or less	1 T. dough enhancer

In a large mixing bowl, put in water, eggs, dough enhancer, yeast, and 4 c. flour. Beat thoroughly with wire whisk or egg beater. Let stand 15 minutes until it has risen in a sponge. Then add rest of ingredients and knead 10-15 minutes using enough flour to make a soft dough. Let rise once, then put out in 4 pans. Let rise again. Bake at 350° for 30 minutes. Yields 4 loaves.

Mrs. John (Loma) Kauffman

100% Whole Wheat Bread

2 eggs	2 T. wheat gluten (heaping)
4¼ c. water	2 T. yeast (heaping)
1 c. oil	1 T. lecithin (heaping)
2 T. salt	11 c. organic wheat flour
¾ c. honey	

Mix well in order given. Mix gluten and yeast with some of the flour. Bake at 350° for 30 minutes. Yield: 4 loaves.

Mrs. Ernest (Mary Ellen) Miller

Rice and Tapioca Bread

½ c. warm water
2 tsp. sugar
4 tsp. dry yeast
1½ c. warm water
4 eggs
4 T. oil
1 T. lemon juice

2 c. tapioca flour
2 c. rice flour
⅔ c. powdered milk
4 tsp. xanthan gum
1½ tsp. salt
¼ c. sugar

Mix first 3 ingredients together. Let set until yeast is dissolved. Mix in remaining ingredients. Let rise one hour. Make rolls, cinnamon rolls, or loaves. Makes wheat and gluten-free bread. Xanthan gum can be found at a health food store.

Mrs. Edna Slabaugh

Heidelberg Rye Bread

2¼ c. whole wheat flour
¼ c. carob powder
2 T. yeast
1 T. caraway seeds
2 c. water

½ c. molasses
2 T. butter
1 tsp. salt
2½ c. rye flour

Combine whole wheat flour, carob powder, yeast, and caraway seeds. Heat water, molasses, butter, and salt in a saucepan until very warm. Beat into flour mixture until smooth. Add enough rye flour to make a slightly stiff dough. Knead about 10 minutes, adding more rye flour if needed. Cover and let rest 20 minutes. Divide in half and shape into 2 round loaves about 6 inches across. Place on greased cookie sheet (or in pie pans) and slash tops with sharp knife or razor blade. Brush with oil and let rise until doubled, about 1 hour. Bake at 350° for 45-50 minutes or until loaves sound hollow when tapped. Cool on racks and refrigerate.

Mrs. Elvie (Rebekah) Miller

The only people you should try to get even with are the ones who have helped you.

Rye Bread

6 c. warm water
6 T. yeast (instant)
1½ c. honey
¾ c. oil
3 T. salt

3 T. lecithin
3 c. whole wheat flour
8 c. rye flour
6 c. white flour

Mix first 6 ingredients in a 13-qt. mixing bowl. Next mix whole wheat flour and rye flour in with a spoon. Work the white flour in with your hands, 1 or 2 c. at a time. Dough should be elastic-like and pull away from bowl. If it doesn't, add a little more white flour. Makes 5 loaves.

Mrs. Monroe (Elsie) Miller

Molly's Bread

2 c. oatmeal
1 to 2 T. salt
½ to 1 c. honey (or sugar)
3½ c. boiling water
4 eggs

1½ c. warm water
2 T. yeast
2 T. sugar
3 to 4 c. wheat flour

Pour boiling water over oatmeal, salt, and honey. Let cool for about 20-30 minutes, until just warm. Mix warm water, yeast, and sugar and let stand until foamy. Add eggs to oatmeal mixture; now add yeast mixture. Stir; add wheat flour. Then add more white or brown flour. Let rise. Punch down, shape into loaves, and let rise again. Bake at 425° for 5 minutes, then at 350° until done. Makes 3-4 loaves.

Mrs. Leroy (Viola) Mast

Bread

4 c. warm water
2 T. yeast
¼ c. honey, molasses, or
    maple syrup

3 tsp. salt
3 T. salad oil
11½ c. whole wheat flour, freshly
    ground from hard wheat

Dissolve sweetener in warm water. Add yeast and 5 cups flour. Beat well until batter is smooth and stretchy. Let set until it begins to rise only a little bit. Add salt and oil. Beat well. Add the rest of the flour, one cup at a time. After it is all mixed, keep on kneading dough for several minutes. Spread a pat of softened butter over the top of the dough. Mix it in well with your hand. Turn dough over and repeat. Let rise for 20 minutes. Punch down dough and divide into 3 loaves. Allow to rise in pans for 30 minutes. Bake at 350° for 30 minutes.

Mrs. Freeman (Wilma) Troyer

Sandwich Buns

2 c. warm water
½ c. melted butter
2 T. yeast
½ c. honey

1 T. salt
2 eggs, well beaten
6½ to 7 c. whole wheat flour

In mixing bowl, add all ingredients except flour. Beat well. Add 3 cups flour; stir until smooth. Add remaining flour. Knead and place in greased bowl. Cover; let rise until double. Punch down; let rise again. Shape into rolls. Place in greased pans and let rise. Bake at 350° for 25 minutes.

Mrs. Omer (Martha) Miller

Bran Muffins

¾ c. whole wheat flour
½ c. wheat germ
½ c. All-Bran cereal
¼ c. oil (scant)
½ c. boiling water
1 c. buttermilk

½ c. oatmeal
½ c. rye flour
¼ c. honey
½ tsp. salt
1 egg, beaten
1¼ tsp. baking soda

Combine dry ingredients; add the rest of the ingredients and mix well. Bake at 400° for 20 minutes.

Mrs. Nathan (Mattie) Miller

Waffles

2 c. whole wheat flour, freshly
   ground hard red winter wheat
2 tsp. baking powder
½ tsp. salt

3 eggs, separated
1½ c. milk
¼ c. melted shortening

Combine flour, baking powder, and salt; stir to mix. Beat egg whites. Set aside. Beat egg yolks; add milk and shortening. Add all at once to flour mixture and beat until dry ingredients are moistened. Fold in egg whites. Bake in preheated waffle iron until done. Makes 6 7-inch waffles.

Mrs. Freeman (Wilma) Troyer

Pancakes

2 c. whole wheat flour	3 tsp. baking powder
1 c. cornmeal	⅔ c. salad oil
1 tsp. salt	3 eggs
1 tsp. soda	3 c. milk

Stir well to mix. Let set a few minutes while you heat a skillet. Lightly grease the skillet and fry.

Mrs. Freeman (Wilma) Troyer

Pancakes

½ c. whole wheat flour	2 T. sweetener (raw sugar, honey,
½ c. white flour	fructose, or maple syrup)
2 tsp. baking powder	¾ c. milk (or until right consistency)
½ tsp. salt	2 T. oil
1 egg, beaten	

Beat all together with egg beater. Our favorite; never flops and very good! Serves 2.

Mrs. Dewayne (Edna Sue) Miller

Cornmeal Pancakes

2 c. whole wheat flour	½ tsp. salt
1 c. cornmeal	2 eggs
1 tsp. baking soda	2½ c. buttermilk
Syrup:	
1 part brown sugar	maple flavor
1 part water	

Mix all together and fry on lightly greased griddle. You may add more milk for thinner cakes or less for fat cakes. Makes 12-16 pancakes. Boil syrup ingredients together. Serve hot.

Mrs. John Almon (Elmina) Mast

The only food that doesn't get expensive is food for thought.

The Authentic Amish Cookbook

Whole Wheat Pancakes

¾ c. whole wheat flour
½ tsp. salt
1 T. sugar
1 tsp. baking powder

½ tsp. baking soda
1 egg
1 c. buttermilk or sour milk

Mix dry ingredients; add egg. Gradually add milk. Mix well. Bake on greased griddle. Griddle needs to be greased only once. (If you don't have sour milk, add 2 T. vinegar to 1 cup milk.)

Mrs. Joe (Susie) Delagrange

Whole Grain Pancake Mix

3 c. whole wheat flour
2½ c. rye or buckwheat flour
½ c. oatmeal
1 c. wheat germ

1 c. cornmeal
5 T. baking powder
1 T. salt
2 T. lecithin

Store mix in refrigerator. To make pancakes, use:

1 c. milk
1 egg

¼ c. oil
1½ c. mix

Combine milk, egg, and oil. Add to mix and stir just until mixed. Bake on griddle.

Mrs. Wilbur (Joann) Hochstetler

Oatmeal Pancakes

2¼ c. oatmeal
2 tsp. baking powder
1 tsp. soda
2 T. honey

2 egg yolks
¼ c. melted butter or oil
egg whites

Soak oatmeal overnight in milk or water. Next morning add next 5 ingredients and blend well. Beat egg whites until stiff and fold into batter. Batter will be thick. Grease griddle lightly. These pancakes require careful baking and flipping but are delicious! Good cold as a snack!

Mrs. Elvie (Rebekah) Miller

Wheat Germ Crunchies

3 c. oatmeal	3 eggs
2 c. whole wheat flour	3 tsp. baking powder
2 c. brown sugar	2 tsp. cinnamon
2 c. coconut	1½ tsp. vanilla
1½ c. margarine or butter	1½ tsp. maple flavor
1 c. wheat germ	1 tsp. salt
1 c. wheat bran	1 c. oat bran

Mix all together and bake in 2 regular size cookie sheets 15-20 minutes. Crumble and dry for a while. Store in an airtight container.

Mrs. Wilbur (Joann) Hochstetler

Granola

10 c. oatmeal	3 sticks margarine
1 c. coconut	1 tsp. salt
1 c. sunflower seeds	2 c. brown sugar
1 c. slivered almonds	1½ c. peanut butter
1 c. wheat germ	

Mix dry ingredients. Set aside. Melt margarine, then add salt, peanut butter, and brown sugar. Stir until dissolved. Remove from heat and add to dry ingredients. Spread on cookie sheet and bake in 250° oven until golden brown. Stir frequently. Store in an airtight container.

Rosanna Yoder

Peanut Butter Granola

10 c. oatmeal	½ c. oil or margarine
2 c. wheat germ	½ c. honey
2 c. coconut	2 tsp. vanilla
1½ c. brown sugar	1 tsp. salt
nuts and raisins	½ c. peanut butter

Heat oil, honey, and peanut butter until lukewarm, then stir together. Mix rest of ingredients; add oil mixture and mix well. Pour into pans. Toast in 270° oven until golden brown, stirring occasionally. Coconut and raisins may be added after it is baked.

Keturah Engbretson

Grapenuts

9 c. wheat flour
2 c. brown sugar
¾ T. salt
1 T. baking soda

¾ c. margarine, melted
2 tsp. vanilla
5 c. buttermilk or sour milk

Put in bowl in order given; mix well. The thickness varies a little with your own wheat flour or store-bought flour. The dough should be fairly thick. If it is too thick, I add a little more milk, and if not thick enough, add more flour until the right consistency. Put in pans and spread evenly with spoon or spatula. Bake in 350° oven until done.

Mrs. Leroy (Viola) Mast

Grapenuts

8 lb. whole wheat flour
5 lb. brown sugar
1¼ T. salt
2½ qt. buttermilk or sour milk

4 tsp. baking soda
¾ lb. margarine, melted
2 T. vanilla
1½ tsp. maple flavor

Put dry ingredients in bowl except soda, which should be added to milk just before adding the milk to dry ingredients. Last, add margarine and flavorings; mix well. The thickness varies a little with your own whole wheat flour or store-bought flour. The dough should be thick. If it's too thick, add a little more milk. Divide into 4 9 x 13-inch pans and spread evenly. Bake in 350° oven until done. Crumble and spread in pans to dry in oven at 225°. Stir every 15 minutes.

Mrs. Wilmer (Clara Mae) Yoder

Corn Crunch Cereal

1 qt. buttermilk or sour milk
3 c. cornmeal
2 c. brown sugar or
　1 c. maple syrup

2 tsp. salt
2 tsp. baking soda
2 tsp. baking powder
4 c. whole wheat flour

Mix all dry ingredients. Stir in milk. Spread on greased cookie sheets. Bake at 350° for 35 minutes. Cool, then put through grapenut screen or Salad Master. Put on cookie sheets and toast in oven until golden brown, like grapenuts.

Mrs. John (Loma) Kauffman

The Authentic Amish Cookbook

Pies, Cakes, and Cookies

Hier auf Erden bin ich ein Pilger

Mrs. M.S.B.D. Shindler, geb. 1810
Übers. Anon.

Italienische Melodie

1. Hier auf Er - den bin ich ein Pil - ger, Und mein Pil-gern, und mein
2. Wo die Son - ne auf im - mer schei-net, O wie sehn' ich, o wie
3. In dem Lan - de, zu dem ich ge - he, Mein Er - lö - ser, mein Er -

Pil - gern währt nicht lang; O lass mich zie - hen zu je - nen Hö - hen,
sehn' ich mich da - hin! Ich bin ein Wand'-rer in frem-den Lan-den,
lö - ser ist das Licht. Da ist kein Kum-mer und kein Ver - der - ben,

REFRAIN

Wo Frie-dens - pal - men auf e - wig we - hen! Hier auf Er - den bin
Mein Herz ist trau - rig, mein Geist in Ban - den.
Da ist kein Ir - ren, und auch kein Ster - ben.

ich ein Pil - ger, Und mein Pil-gern, und mein Pil - gern währt nicht lang.

Sugar-Free Oatmeal Pie

3 beaten eggs	¼ c. quick oats
⅓ c. honey	½ c. coconut
½ c. molasses	¾ to 1 c. milk
2 T. browned butter	1 tsp. vanilla
½ tsp. maple flavoring	¼ tsp. cinnamon

Blend together and pour into unbaked pie shell. Bake at 350° for 30-35 minutes.

Mrs. Dewayne (Edna Sue) Miller

Tofu Maple Cheesecake

⅓ c. orange juice concentrate	⅔ c. maple syrup
1 T. unflavored gelatin	½ tsp. vanilla
2 12-oz. bars or 2 10.5-oz. pkg. tofu	2 T. lemon juice
1 large ripe banana	1½ c. rolled oats

Dissolve gelatin in ¼ c. cold water. Heat orange juice concentrate over low heat and add gelatin. Cool. Blend rest of ingredients (except oats) in blender, then add orange juice concentrate and blend well. (A Salsa Master could also be used.) For crust, use rolled oats and add enough of the filling to make it stick together. Press into pie pan and pour in filling. You can chop a little flaxseed and sprinkle on top if you wish. Refrigerate several hours or overnight. A graham cracker or butter crunch crust can also be used. Serves 4-6.

Mrs. Elvie (Rebekah) Miller

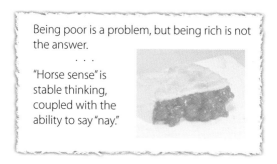

Being poor is a problem, but being rich is not the answer.

. . .

"Horse sense" is stable thinking, coupled with the ability to say "nay."

Whole Wheat Cocoa Chiffon Cake

½ c. cocoa
¾ c. boiling water
7 to 8 eggs, separated
½ c. salad oil
1 tsp. vanilla

1 tsp. salt
1½ c. sugar
3 tsp. baking powder
1¾ c. whole wheat flour

Stir cocoa and boiling water together until smooth. Separate eggs until there is 1 c. whites. Set yolks aside. Beat whites until stiff. Mix together flour, salt, sugar, and baking powder. Make a well and add oil, egg yolks, cocoa mixture, and vanilla; mix. Pour this mixture over egg whites; fold gently. Bake at 350° in 10-inch tube pan until done.

Regina Miller

Banana Nut Cake

⅔ c. mashed bananas
½ c. softened butter
3 eggs
¾ c. water
2 c. whole wheat flour

2 tsp. baking powder
1 tsp. baking soda
1 tsp. cinnamon
1 c. nuts
¾ c. raisins

Mix first 3 ingredients together well. Add rest of ingredients. Pour into 13 x 9 x 2-inch cake pan, greased and floured. Bake at 350° for 35 minutes.

Mrs. Omer (Martha) Miller

Zucchini Fudge Cake

4 eggs
¾ c. maple syrup
2 tsp. vanilla
¾ c. butter or oil
3 c. whole wheat flour
½ c. carob powder
2 tsp. cinnamon

2 tsp. baking powder
1 tsp. baking soda
¾ tsp. salt
1 c. buttermilk
3 c. shredded zucchini, unpeeled
1 c. chopped walnuts

Beat first 4 ingredients well. Combine dry ingredients. Stir ½ of dry ingredients into egg mixture. Add buttermilk; mix well. Add remaining flour mixture and mix. Fold in zucchini and walnuts. Pour into 9 x 13-inch pan. Bake at 350° for 45-50 minutes or until top springs back when gently touched.

Beth Ann Yoder

Pumpkin Cake

2 eggs
1 c. cooked pumpkin
¾ c. honey (can be substituted
  with brown sugar)
½ c. oil
½ tsp. salt
1 tsp. baking soda

2 tsp. baking powder
1 tsp. cinnamon
½ tsp. nutmeg
¼ tsp. ginger
¼ tsp. cloves
⅔ c. water or milk
1½ c. whole wheat flour

Beat eggs in a bowl. Add rest of ingredients except the last two. Mix well. Add the water or milk and flour; mix well. Bake at 350° to 375°.

Mrs. Kenneth (Martha) Miller

Nutritious and Delicious Carrot Cake

1 c. vegetable oil
¾ c. honey
3 eggs
1 tsp. vanilla
½ tsp. salt
2 c. whole wheat flour
2 tsp. baking soda
  Maple Cream Cheese Icing:
2 8-oz. pkg. cream cheese

2 tsp. baking powder
2 tsp. cinnamon
2 c. shredded carrots
1 medium apple, finely diced
½ c. raisins
½ c. unsweetened coconut
½ c. pecans or walnuts, chopped

maple syrup

Beat first five ingredients vigorously for 3-5 minutes in a large mixing bowl. In another bowl combine flour, baking soda, baking powder, and cinnamon. Mix into liquid ingredients. Add carrots, apple, raisins, coconut, and nuts and stir into batter. Bake in greased 9 x 13-inch cake pan at 325° for 35-40 minutes. Cool, then frost with cream cheese icing. Whip cream cheese until smooth. Add enough maple syrup until it's of spreading consistency.

Anna Yoder

A lot of kneeling keeps you in good standing with God.

Strawberry Shortcake

4 c. whole wheat flour	6 tsp. baking powder
1 tsp. salt	4 T. maple syrup
1½ c. milk	½ c. butter

Bake at 425° for 20 minutes. Serve with milk and strawberries.

Mrs. Mahlon (Wanita Kay) Bontrager

Carob Cake

3¼ c. whole wheat pastry flour	2 T. vinegar
2 tsp. baking soda	2 tsp. vanilla
¾ c. oil	1¾ c. honey
1⅔ c. water	6 T. carob powder

Blend dry ingredients; mix rest of ingredients and combine both. Bake 35 minutes at 350°.

You can also bake this on a cookie sheet, and then thicken and sweeten (if you want) a quart of cherries. Spread cherries over cake instead of icing and sprinkle with unsweetened shredded coconut.

Mrs. Nathan (Mattie) Miller

Coconut Oatmeal Cookies

¾ c. butter	1 c. coconut
¼ c. raw sugar	¼ c. wheat germ
½ c. maple syrup	1 tsp. baking powder
2 eggs	1 tsp. baking soda
1 c. whole wheat flour	1½ c. raisins
1 c. oatmeal	

Cream butter, sugars, and eggs together thoroughly. Add flour, oats, coconut, wheat germ, baking powder, and soda. Mix well. Stir in raisins. Drop by spoonfuls onto lightly greased baking sheets. Flatten slightly with floured fork. Bake at 350° for 12-15 minutes or until light golden. Makes 36 cookies.

Mrs. David (Rhoda) Miller

The Authentic Amish Cookbook

Whole Wheat Cookies

½ c. butter, softened
½ c. peanut butter
½ c. honey
1 egg
1 tsp. vanilla

1 c. whole wheat flour
½ c. nonfat dry milk powder
½ c. wheat germ
1 tsp. baking soda

In a mixing bowl, cream butter, peanut butter, and honey. Beat in egg and vanilla. In another bowl, combine the remaining ingredients; add to the creamed mixture. Cover and refrigerate for 30 minutes. Drop by teaspoonfuls 2 inches apart onto ungreased baking sheet. Flatten with fork dipped in raw sugar. Bake at 350° for 8-10 minutes or until golden brown. Let cool on pan for 1 minute before removing to wire racks to cool completely. Makes 3 dozen.

Mrs. Omer (Martha) Miller

Chocolate Chip Cookies

4 c. brown sugar
1½ c. softened butter
4 eggs
1 tsp. baking powder
2 tsp. baking soda
1 tsp. salt

2 tsp. vanilla
4½ c. whole wheat flour
4 c. oatmeal
2 c. chocolate chips
2 c. walnuts

Cream together sugar and butter. Blend in eggs. Add the rest of the ingredients, mixing well. Bake on ungreased cookie sheet for 8-10 minutes at 400°. These cookies are better if they are slightly underbaked rather than overbaked.

Mrs. Freeman (Wilma) Troyer

The will of God will
not lead you where
the grace of God
cannot keep you.

Whole Wheat Cut-Out Cookies

¾ c. shortening
¾ c. brown sugar
2 eggs
¼ tsp. salt

1 tsp. vanilla
2 c. whole wheat flour
1 tsp. baking powder
1 tsp. baking soda

Cream shortening and sugar; stir in eggs and vanilla. Add the dry ingredients and mix well. Roll thinly and cut out. Bake at 350° until browned. May be pasted together with jam or icing, but are also good plain.

Mrs. Nathan (Mattie) Miller

Sesame Sun Refrigerator Cookies (Slice and Bake)

½ c. butter, softened
½ c. honey
1 egg
1 tsp. vanilla
¾ c. whole wheat flour

1½ c. rolled oats
¼ c. wheat germ
½ tsp. baking soda
¾ c. sunflower seeds
¾ c. sesame seeds

Cream butter, honey, egg, and vanilla. Mix dry ingredients and mix with cream mixture along with seeds. Shape dough into 2 logs about 2 inches in diameter. Wrap in wax paper. Refrigerate 4 hours or freeze 2 hours. Cut in ¼-inch slices. Place on ungreased cookie sheet. Bake at 375° for 10 minutes. Makes 4 dozen.

Mrs. Jerry (Ruth) Gingerich

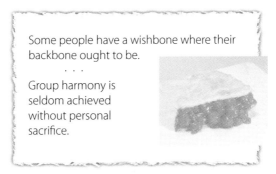

Some people have a wishbone where their backbone ought to be.

. . .

Group harmony is seldom achieved without personal sacrifice.

The Authentic Amish Cookbook

Oatmeal Fruit Cookies

1 c. flour
¼ tsp. cloves
1 tsp. baking soda
½ tsp. cinnamon
1 c. apple juice

½ c. chopped apples
½ c. butter
½ c. raisins
½ c. chopped dates
1 c. quick oatmeal

Bring juice, dates, apples, butter, raisins, and oatmeal to a boil. Simmer 3 minutes. Remove from heat and stir into sifted dry mixture until well blended. Cool. Cover and refrigerate overnight. Drop by teaspoonfuls 2 inches apart on greased baking sheet. Bake at 350° for 10-14 minutes.

Mrs. John Almon (Elmina) Mast

Carob No-Bake Cookies

2 c. brown sugar
4 T. carob powder
½ c. milk
½ c. margarine or butter

½ c. peanut butter
1 tsp. vanilla
3 c. oatmeal

Mix the sugar, carob powder, milk, and margarine together in saucepan. Boil for 1 minute. Add peanut butter and vanilla; mix well. Add the oatmeal and drop by teaspoonfuls on cookie sheet and put in the refrigerator.

You can also use 1 c. honey instead of sugar and reduce the milk a little; it will be stickier. You may add raisins, nuts, or whatever you choose.

Mrs. Nathan (Mattie) Miller

Sunflower Bars

2 c. sunflower seeds
1 c. sesame seeds
1 c. unsweetened coconut
⅓ c. peanut butter

⅓ c. honey, thin or slightly warm
1 tsp. vanilla
½ tsp. maple flavoring

You can substitute chopped almonds for sesame seeds. Mix and press into pan and chill a few hours or overnight.

Mrs. David (Rhoda) Miller

Flaxseed Bars

6 c. flaxseed, freshly ground
1 c. honey
1 c. peanut butter
1 c. nuts

1 c. carob chips
1 tsp. vanilla
1 tsp. maple flavoring

Thoroughly mix flaxseed, honey, peanut butter, and flavorings. To make mixing easier, heat honey, peanut butter, and flavorings over low heat, stirring constantly, until just warm. Then mix well with ground flaxseed. Last add nuts and carob chips. Press into a greased 9 x 13-inch pan and chill several hours or overnight. Cut into bars. Flaxseed can be ground in a blender. Makes 24 bars.

Mrs. Elvie (Rebekah) Miller
Mrs. Jonas (Elizabeth) Wagler

Honey Whole Wheat Chip Bars

3 c. whole wheat flour
1½ tsp. baking powder
½ tsp. soda
½ tsp. salt
1 c. butter

1 c. honey
3 eggs
2 tsp. vanilla
¾ c. chocolate, carob, or
    butterscotch chips

Stir together first 4 ingredients. Add melted butter and honey. Mix well. Add eggs, vanilla, and chocolate chips and mix well. Bake in hot oven. Watch closely and do not overbake. Cut into bars while hot.

Mrs. Wilbur (Joann) Hochstetler

Sesame Seed Squares

½ c. honey
½ c. peanut butter
1 c. sesame seeds

1 c. powdered milk
½ c. coconut

Heat honey and peanut butter until peanut butter is melted. Add dry milk, coconut, and then seeds. Mix and pat into 8-inch square pan. Refrigerate to set. Cut into squares.

Mrs. John (Loma) Kauffman

Full of Energy Bars

2 c. whole wheat flour	½ c. chopped dried apricots,
½ c. brown sugar	optional
¼ c. skim milk powder	½ c. unsalted sunflower seeds
¼ c. wheat germ	2 eggs
1 tsp. baking powder	½ c. molasses
1 c. raisins	½ c. water

Combine dry ingredients. Mix remaining ingredients and add to dry ingredients, mixing well. Spread in greased 9-inch square pan. Bake 35 minutes at 350°. Cool. Cut into bars.

Mrs. Nathan (Mattie) Miller

Peanut Butter Bars

2 c. whole wheat flour	1 c. peanut butter
2 c. oat bran	1 c. sorghum
1 c. wheat bran	2 T. vanilla
1¼ tsp. salt	½ c. apple butter or sauce

Stir salt and peanut butter together. In a separate bowl, stir together the sorghum, vanilla, and apple butter. Stir both mixtures and the first 3 ingredients together well. Press dough onto cookie sheet. Bake at 350° for 30 minutes and cut while still warm.

Mrs. Alva (Elnora) Hochstetler

Double Delight

¾ c. oatmeal	¼ c. raisins
¼ c. honey	1 c. butter
2 tsp. baking powder	½ tsp. salt
1 c. carob chips	1 egg
1 c. flour	

Combine all ingredients in bowl. Spread batter evenly in greased 10 x 15-inch pan. Bake at 350° for 25-30 minutes or until golden brown.

Mrs. Edna Slabaugh

Matrimony Squares

Crumbs:

2 c. oatmeal   ½ c. honey
2 c. wheat flour   ½ tsp. salt
1 c. butter
  Filling:
3 c. dates   1 tsp. vanilla
½ c. honey   water to cover

Cook filling until well thickened. Set aside to cool. Mix crumbs. Press ¾ of crumbs into bottom of 9 x 13-inch pan. Spread filling on top of crumbs. Sprinkle remaining crumbs on top. Bake until nicely browned. Note: 1½ qt. well-thickened and sweetened cooked fruit may be used instead of dates. Blueberry is good!

Mrs. Dewayne (Edna Sue) Miller

Consider the pin. . .
its head keeps it
from going too far.

Main Dishes

My Ways Are Not Your Ways

Isaiah 55:8

Barbara Nichols

Marvin Nichols
Marjorie Nichols

1. Oft the way to the goal seems so wea-ry and long, Tri-als al-most
2. It is my heart's de-sire to do His bless-ed will, And to serve my
3. So I'll leave all to Him, He has prom-ised to share All my load and

take a-way our song; Then we sigh and we cry and we ask, "Fa-ther, why
Mas-ter ev-'ry day; But when things all go wrong and the world doubts me still
ev-'ry care to bear. There is joy in my heart and on my lips a song,

Chorus

Does this life my wish-es all de-ny?"
Then, oh Lord, I can-not un-der-stand. My ways, my child, are not
E-ven tho, Lord, I don't un-der-stand.

your ways, My tho'ts are high-er than thine. Let me lead you each

step of this long wea-ry day, Let me clasp thy trem-bling hand in Mine.

Sausage-Apple Stuffed Squash

3 large acorn squash, halved and seeded
1½ lb. pork sausage meat
¾ c. oats
½ tsp. salt
½ c. chopped apple
¼ c. chopped onion
1 T. finely chopped parsley
½ c. milk

Place squash cut side down in shallow baking pan. Pour a little water in pan. Bake in preheated 350° oven about 30 minutes. While squash is baking, make sausage balls. Combine sausage, oats, salt, apple, onion, parsley, and milk thoroughly. Shape to form 18 sausage balls. Brown lightly in small amount of shortening in large skillet. Remove squash from oven; turn cut side up. Season with salt and pepper. Place 3 sausage balls in center of each squash. Continue to bake 40 minutes or until squash is tender. Serves 6.

Lena Yoder

Ham Vegetable Scallop

1 10½-oz. can cream of
mushroom soup
½ c. milk
⅓ c. finely chopped onion
2 c. diced potatoes
1 c. sliced carrots
1 10-oz. pkg. lima beans
1½ c. cooked and cut ham
½ c. buttered bread crumbs

Mix soup and milk; heat to boiling while stirring. Add vegetables alternately with ham to fill greased 1½-quart casserole. Add soup. Sprinkle bread crumbs over the top. Make cup-shaped hole in center; line with thin ham slices. Border with ham strips. Bake 1 hour at 350°. Tuck crisp sprigs of parsley into ham cup before serving. Serves 6.

Lena Yoder

"I sought the Lord, and he heard me, and delivered me from all my fears." Psalm 34:4

Chicken and Spinach Omelet

½ c. egg
2 oz. chicken, diced
10 c. spinach
4 c. sliced mushrooms
3 c. bean sprouts
1½ c. onions, diced
1⅓ tsp. olive oil, divided

1 T. soy sauce
½ tsp. Worcestershire sauce
2 T. vinegar
⅛ tsp. chili powder
⅛ tsp. cayenne pepper
⅛ tsp. celery salt

Heat 1 tsp. oil in a medium nonstick sauté pan. Sauté chicken and onion until lightly browned. Add spinach, mushrooms, and bean sprouts. Cook 3-5 minutes. Add remaining oil to another sauté pan. In small bowl stir soy sauce, Worcestershire sauce, vinegar, and seasoning into egg, then pour into sauté pan. Cook until almost set. Spoon vegetables onto half of omelette. Fold over and cook 1 additional minute. Serves 2.

Lena Yoder

Lentil Burgers

2 c. raw lentils
5 c. water
1 c. quick oats
1 small onion
½ c. catsup

2 eggs
1 tsp. garlic powder
  and/or other seasoning
whole wheat flour

Bring water and lentils to boil. Simmer until lentils have absorbed nearly all the water. Mix lentils together with remaining ingredients. Form into patties, using enough flour so they keep their shape. Broil in oven or fry in pan like hamburgers.

Mrs. John (Fannie) Miller

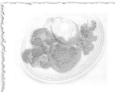

Distrust is to marriage
as termites are to an
old frame building.

Taco-Filled Baked Squash

1 halved squash, butternut, summer
  squash, or your favorite kind
1 T. taco seasoning
cheese

½ to 1 lb. buffalo burger or
  lean hamburger
½ c. salsa, optional

Remove seeds from squash. Brown meat and add rest of ingredients. Fill hollow of squash with meat and bake in baking dish for 1½-2 hours. Add shredded cheese on top for the last 5 minutes of baking. Serves 2-4.

Mrs. Wilbur (Joann) Hochstetler

Fish Fillets with Lemon and Parsley

1 lb. fish fillets
salt
freshly ground pepper
2 tsp. butter, melted

2 T. chopped parsley
1 T. lemon juice,
  fresh lemons are best

Place fillets in lightly oiled baking dish just large enough to hold them in a single layer. Sprinkle with salt and pepper to taste. Combine butter, parsley, and lemon juice. Drizzle over fish. Bake uncovered at 450° for 10 minutes per inch thickness for fresh fish. Add 5 minutes if fish is wrapped in foil and double the time if fish is still frozen. Perfectly cooked fish is opaque and flakes slightly. Avoid overcooking; it dries out the fish.

Mrs. David (Rhoda) Miller

Cashew Nut Casserole

1 c. cashew nuts, chopped
1 c. onion, chopped
1 c. mushrooms, chopped
1 c. celery, chopped
2 T. oil
1 c. dry egg noodles (fine)

1 tsp. Accent seasoning
1 c. dry Chinese noodles, optional
1 c. liquid from mushrooms (add
  water to make 1 c. if needed)
½ tsp. salt

Mix all together. Bake 1 hour at 350°. Each serving is 235 calories. Serves 6.

Mrs. Roy (Martha) Hershberger

Rice Croquettes

½ c. chopped onion
2 T. butter
1 c. uncooked brown rice
2¼ c. chicken broth
2 T. fresh parsley
1 egg

½ c. cheese
1 tsp. dried basil
¼ tsp. pepper
½ c. dry bread crumbs or oat bran,
   wheat bran, cornmeal, etc.

Sauté onion in butter until tender; add rice. Sauté 3 minutes. Stir in broth and parsley and bring to a boil. Reduce heat, cover, and simmer 40 minutes. Cool and stir in egg, cheese, basil, and pepper. Shape into logs and roll in crumbs and fry in olive oil. You can also sprinkle crumbs onto hot oil and drop spoonfuls on top, flattening into patties and sprinkling tops with crumbs before turning.

Mrs. David (Rhoda) Miller

Chinese Glob

1 lb. hamburger
1 c. chopped celery
1 c. brown rice

1 c. chopped onions
1 qt. whole wheat gravy

Cook rice and fry hamburger and onions together. Then mix all ingredients and season to taste. Bake for 1 hour at 350°.

Mrs. Earl (Irma) Chupp

Shake and Bake

5 c. whole wheat flour
1¼ c. wheat germ
3½ T. seasoned salt

½ c. salt
2½ tsp. pepper
5 tsp. celery salt

Mix ingredients together. Roll chicken in mixture. Drizzle a little melted butter over chicken and bake at 350° until tender.

Mrs. Jerome (Rose) Graber

"Out of the abundance of the heart the mouth speaketh." Matthew 12:34

Burger Delight

2 c. bulgur wheat
1 c. water
1 c. tomato juice
½ medium onion, cut in pieces

1 garlic clove
1 c. walnuts
2 T. Vege-sal
2 T. sorghum

Place bulgur in a saucepan. Put all other ingredients in a blender and blend until smooth. Stir blended ingredients into saucepan. Cook over medium heat for about 15 minutes or until thickened, stirring frequently. Spread mixture evenly on a lightly oiled cookie sheet (with sides) and bake at 250° for 45-60 minutes, stirring occasionally until it has a crumbly consistency. Remove from oven while still moist. Can be bagged and frozen by the pound for easy use. This is so great to use as a pizza topping, or add tomato sauce for a sloppy joe sandwich filling. It's also great in spaghetti, soups, casseroles, stirred into rice, or as a baked potato topper. Try it, you'll like it!

Mrs. John (Rosanna) Bowman

Pita Pizza

whole wheat pita bread
pizza sauce
mozzarella cheese

assorted vegetables
pepperoni
sausage, hamburger

Lay pitas on baking sheet. Spread with pizza sauce. Layer on vegetables and meat. Top with cheese. Broil a few minutes until golden brown.

Mrs. John (Rosanna) Bowman

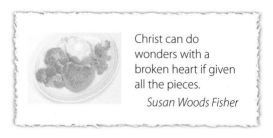

Christ can do wonders with a broken heart if given all the pieces.

Susan Woods Fisher

Notes

Desserts

His Yoke Is Easy

My yoke is easy, and my burden is light. —Matthew 11:30

Daniel S. Warner, 1842-1895　　　　　　　　　B. Elliott Warren, 1867-1951

1. I've found my Lord and He is mine, He won me by His love;
2. No oth - er Lord but Christ I know, I walk with Him a - lone;
3. He's dear - er to my heart than life, He found me lost in sin;
4. My flesh re - coiled be - fore the cross, And Sa - tan whis-pered there,
5. I've tried the road of sin and found Its pros-pects all de - ceive;

I'll serve Him all my years of time, And dwell with Him a - bove.
His streams of love for - ev - er flow, With-in my heart, His throne.
He calmed the sea of in-ward strife, And bade me come to Him.
"Thy gain will not re - pay the loss, His yoke is hard to bear."
I've proved the Lord and joys a-bound, More than I could be - lieve.

REFRAIN

His yoke is eas - y, His bur-den is light, I've found it so, I've found it so;

His service is my sweetest de-light, His bless-ings ev - er flow.

Baked Oatmeal

2 eggs, beaten
½ c. olive oil
½ c. honey or maple syrup
3 c. oatmeal

1 tsp. salt
½ tsp. baking powder
1 c. milk

Mix all ingredients together. Pour into a greased 9-inch baking dish. Bake at 350° for 40-45 minutes. Serve warm with milk or whipped cream. Optional: I add raisins, diced apples, cinnamon, nuts, or coconut—one or several of these—and use it as a dessert. Delicious! Serves 6-8.

Mrs. Ben (Keturah) Troyer

Fruit Crunch Dessert

¾ c. brown sugar
½ c. soft margarine
1 c. quick oats

1 c. whole wheat flour
½ tsp. salt
½ tsp. baking soda

Put ½ of mixture in 8 x 8-inch pan. Put thickened fruit of your choice on crumbs, and put rest of crumbs on top. Bake 30 minutes at 350°.

Mrs. Nathan (Mattie) Miller

Yogurt

1 gal. milk
2 T. gelatin
½ c. cold water

2 T. vanilla
4 T. plain yogurt
¾ c. maple syrup

Heat milk to 190°. While milk is heating, soak gelatin in water. Add to hot milk and cool to 130°. Then add vanilla, yogurt, and syrup. Beat until smooth and put into containers. Cover and put into oven with just pilot light on for 5 hours. Refrigerate.

Mrs. Loyal (Dorcas) Gingerich

Life's most perplexing problems usually come in the form of people.

Sugar-Free Date Pudding

1 c. chopped dates
1 tsp. baking soda
1 c. boiling water
2 eggs
  Pudding and Cream:
½ pt. whipping cream
½ tsp. vanilla
1 small box sugar-free instant
  butterscotch pudding

1 T. butter
1½ c. whole wheat flour
1 pinch salt
½ c. chopped walnuts

1 pinch salt
1 T. apple juice concentrate

Put soda over dates. Pour boiling water over. Let set until cooled, then add remaining 5 ingredients. Pour into greased 8 x 12-inch pan. Bake at 375° for 25 minutes. Cool.

To make pudding and cream, whip cream; add vanilla, salt, and apple juice concentrate. Mix instant butterscotch pudding mix in blender according to directions on package. At lowest speed on mixer, mix pudding into the cream.

Place in layers in serving dish: date cake cut up in small squares, 2-3 bananas, pudding and cream mixture, ending with pudding and cream on top. Sprinkle chopped nuts over top.

Mrs. Roy (Martha) Hershberger

Sugar-Free Fruit Pizza

½ c. butter
1 egg
1⅓ c. whole grain flour
1 tsp. baking powder
pinch salt

8 oz. cream cheese, softened
1 T. white grape juice concentrate
fresh or canned fruit
2 c. pineapple juice
2 T. gelatin

Cream butter and egg together. Add next 3 ingredients; pat into greased pizza pan. Bake at 375° for 10 minutes. Cool. Cream together cream cheese and grape juice concentrate; spread over cooled crust. Spread fresh or canned fruit all around in circle and covering whole crust. Use pineapple, peaches, pears, bananas, strawberries, blueberries, etc. For glaze, cook pineapple juice and gelatin together until clear. Allow to cool until slightly thickened. Pour over pizza. Refrigerate. Serves 15.

Mrs. Roy (Martha) Hershberger

Whole Wheat Pudding

4¼ c. whole wheat flour
1½ c. sugar
2 eggs
2 c. buttermilk
2 T. shortening
½ tsp. cinnamon

1 tsp. baking soda
2 tsp. baking powder
1 tsp. salt
2 c. raisins
½ tsp. nutmeg

Put dry ingredients in bowl and mix well, then add rest of ingredients and stir well. Add raisins. Put in pans. Bake in 350° oven for 35 minutes or until done. Serve with milk and fruit.

Mrs. Ernest (Sara) Schrock

Peach-Apricot-Raspberry-Blackberry Cobbler

⅓ c. maple syrup
1½ c. water
2 T. cornstarch
   Topping:
½ c. whole wheat flour
¾ tsp. baking powder
2 T. butter, softened

2½ c. fruit, fresh or canned
½ tsp. cinnamon
¼ scant tsp. nutmeg

¼ c. maple syrup
¼ tsp. salt
1 large egg

Bring water and maple syrup to a boil and thicken with cornstarch. Add remaining 3 ingredients. Put fruit sauce mixture in bottom of 1½- or 2-qt. casserole dish, or a flat Pyrex cake pan works also. Top with topping. Bake at 350° for 25-30 minutes or until crust is golden brown.

Mrs. John (Rosanna) Bowman

The gem cannot be polished without friction, nor man be perfected without trials.

Notes

Miscellaneous Recipes

Leave It There

Commit thy way unto the LORD; trust also in him; and he shall bring it to pass. —Psalm 37:5

Charles Albert Tindlay, 1851-1933

Arr. by Charles A. Tindlay, Jr., 20th Century

1. If the world from you withhold of its sil - ver and its gold, And you
2. If your bod - y suf - fers pain and your health you can't re - gain, And your
3. When your en - e - mies as - sail and your heart be - gins to fail, Don't for-
4. When your youthful days are gone and old age is steal - ing on, And your

have to get a - long with meager fare, Just re - mem - ber, in His Word, how He
soul is al - most sink - ing in de - spair, Je - sus knows the pain you feel, He can
get that God in heav - en answers pray'r; He will make a way for you and will
bod - y bends beneath the weight of care; He will nev - er leave you then, He'll go

feeds the lit - tle bird;
save and He can heal;
lead you safe - ly thro';
with you to the end;

FINE REFRAIN

Take your burden to the Lord and leave it there. Leave it

there, leave it there, Take your bur-den to the Lord and leave it
Leave it there, leave it there,

D. S.

there; If you trust and nev - er doubt, He will sure - ly bring you out;
leave it there;

High Fiber Snack

3 c. oatmeal
1 c. peanut butter
½ c. whole wheat flour
¼ tsp. salt

1 c. honey
1 c. chopped nuts or chocolate chips
coconut

Place oatmeal, coconut, nuts, flour, and salt in bowl. Mix well. In another bowl mix together peanut butter and honey. Combine the 2 mixtures and form balls or press in 9 x 13-inch pan and cut in bars. Enjoy!

Mrs. James (Rosanna) Miller

Peanut Butter Balls

½ c. honey
1 c. non-instant powdered milk
  (not made into a liquid)
  Variations:
¼ c. sunflower seeds
¼ c. raisins
¼ c. sesame seeds

½ c. peanut butter
unsweetened coconut

¼ c. walnuts
¼ c. pecans
¼ c. carob

Mix together the honey, peanut butter, and milk powder. Mold into small balls and roll in coconut. Store in refrigerator.

Mrs. Ben (Anna Mary) Fisher

Herb Butter

½ c. butter
½ c. oil
1 T. dried parsley
1½ tsp. basil
¼ tsp. chives

¼ tsp. dried thyme
¼ tsp. salt
⅛ tsp. pepper
⅛ tsp. garlic powder

Put all ingredients in blender or Salsa Master and blend well. Store in refrigerator. Delicious on toast!

Mrs. Elvie (Rebekah) Miller

Let's not overlook life's small joys while looking for the big ones.

"Sugarless" Grape Juice (to can)

Concord grapes   water
maple syrup

Pick grapes off stems and wash. Fill quart jars ¾ full with grapes and add ¼ to ½ c. maple syrup according to sweetness of grapes. Fill with hot water, put lids on, and place in hot water bath for 10-15 minutes. When opening a jar, dilute with ½ qt. water.

Mrs. Wilbur (Joann) Hochstetler

Sugar-Free Pancake Syrup

6-oz. can frozen apple juice or   1 pinch salt
   white grape juice concentrate   1 c. water
⅛ tsp. maple extract   1 T. cornstarch

Mix cornstarch and salt in ½ c. cold water. In saucepan bring juice concentrate and ½ c. water to boil. Stir in cornstarch mixture. Stir constantly; allow to boil a few minutes. Remove from heat. Add maple extract. Serve warm.

Mrs. Roy (Martha) Hershberger

"The Lord is my shepherd; I shall not want."
Psalm 23:1

. . .

The world is filled with beauty when your heart is filled with love.

Tips & Hints

Cooking and Baking

To thicken soup add instant rice or mashed potatoes.

Slip your hand into a waxed sandwich bag and have a perfect mitt for greasing your baking pan.

When cutting meringue-topped pies or puddings, oil the knife or spoon, and then the meringue won't tear or pull.

If you get some egg yolk in egg whites to be beaten, just touch the yolk with a piece of bread. The yolk will adhere to the bread.

Can pumpkins by cutting into chunks (peeled). Put into jars. Fill with water. Pressure can at 10 lb. for 90 minutes (3 hours in boiling water). When ready to use, drain water from jars and mash.

To make baking powder, sift together 2 T. cream of tartar, 1 T. baking soda, and 1 T. cornstarch. Mix well and store in airtight container.

Dip fruit slices in pure lemon juice to keep them from becoming brown.

Egg substitute: 2 T. applesauce

Fill popsicle molds with leftover pudding and freeze. A delicious treat for everyone!

One lemon is equal to 3 to 4 T. lemon juice.

One orange is equal to 6-8 T. orange juice.

Adding unsweetened applesauce or banana to cake or cookie batter will make it more moist. If you use small amounts (¼ to ½ c.), you won't taste it.

Use pastry flour for pie crusts, biscuits, gravy, rivel soup, dumplings, and corn breads.

Peaches have a better flavor if you just stir sugar into them before putting them in jars instead of pouring a syrup on them.

When boiling fresh eggs, crack them very slightly, and they will peel much easier.

Have your cheese well chilled before grating. It will be much easier to grate.

If you want juice for a picnic, freeze in a plastic jug the night before. Put it in your cooler when packing, and it will keep the food cold. The juice will melt enough to pour by picnic time.

Pour salt or baking soda on a small fire to smother it.

When baking, bring eggs to room temperature to make batter lighter and fluffier.

A cooked mashed potato adds moisture to whole grain breads.

Hard-boiled eggs will peel easily when cracked and placed in cold water immediately after taking out of hot water.

Never put fresh pineapple or kiwi into Jell-O because then Jell-O won't thicken.

When boiling water to cook eggs, add a dash of vinegar to prevent them from cracking open.

To keep a cookbook from getting soiled, slide it into a plastic bag.

If melted chocolate is too thick for coating, add a little cooking oil to it.

Separate eggs when taken from refrigerator. Cold yolks are less likely to break than warm ones.

To improve the flavor of green string beans, place an onion in the kettle before adding beans.

Put a piece of bread in the brown sugar container, and the sugar will stay soft.

Leftover Cream of Wheat or oatmeal may be added to hamburger or sausage. Mix thoroughly. Make into patties or a loaf.

Substitute an egg with ½ tsp. baking powder plus 2 T. milk.

Stir milk into leftover cooked cereal or rice before storing. Serve as a dessert by adding whipped cream, apples, raisins, or other raw fruit. An old leftover cake or apple roll may also be added.

To cut fresh bread easily, use a hot knife.

Sweeten whipped cream with powdered sugar if dessert serving is to be delayed. Whip stays fluffy longer than when granulated sugar is used. A touch of plain gelatin also helps to keep it from separating (¼ tsp. per cup of cream).

The crusty tops of homemade bread may be softened by placing a large plastic bag over the loaves as they cool. If you tuck the bag in at the sides, the side crusts will be softened as well.

When baking grapenuts, use flour from soft wheat. The baked cakes will crumble much more easily.

For a deliciously different flavor, stir your cup of hot chocolate with a stick of peppermint candy.

When you have a scorched saucepan, boil a tablespoon or 2 of baking soda and water in it for a while—it will clean easily.

Any saucepan or frying pan will clean easily if you fill it with some water, put a lid on it, and bring it to a boil.

To help maintain quality of canned fruits, use Fruit Fresh by dissolving ¼ tsp. in ¼ c. cold water and adding this to each quart of fruit.

Two tsp. cornstarch added to 1 c. all-purpose flour is equal to 1 c. pastry flour. Sift together 3 times.

By using ¾ c. whole wheat flour for every cup of white flour, you are able to use whole wheat flour in almost any recipe in a cookbook.

Whole grain pasta tends to get sticky after cooking. Do not rinse with cold water. Drain in warmed colander and serve in a warmed dish or add to casserole, meat, soup, etc. and serve. Pasta will also not stick together as readily or boil over if 1 T. oil is added to the cooking water.

Save time each week by sitting down and planning your meals. Using a calendar, list your menu on each day. Each morning check to see what needs to be taken out of the freezer (meat, vegetables). It prevents the stress of trying to quickly decide what to make at 4:00. It also ensures a healthy, balanced meal.

Here's a wonderful way to use leftovers. Keep a bag or container in the freezer to accumulate leftover vegetables, noodles, rice, meat, etc. You can turn out delicious soups and casseroles with these.

For a sweeter finished product in recipes calling for fruit juice, substitute frozen concentrate instead.

Thaw frozen blueberries in thawed strawberries and they won't get mushy; same with frozen black cherries. They're good to eat together and also good with other fruit mixed in.

Cleaning Tips

To remove ink marks from clothing, spray with hair spray.

To remove fly spots from clothing, dab spot with peroxide and iron it with a medium-hot iron.

Use 1 tsp. baking soda to a pint of water to remove stains from plastic kitchenware.

To remove paint spots on clothing, dab on ammonia and turpentine (equal amounts) or peroxide several times, then wash thoroughly.

Bleach keeps countertops nice and clean.

When cooking jars in a hot water bath, add several T. vinegar. This keeps the jars and canners nice and clean. This works well for meat.

To clean windows in cold weather, mix ½ c. ammonia, 1 c. white vinegar, 2 T. cornstarch, ½ c. rubbing alcohol in bucket of warm water. The warm water and alcohol will prevent ice forming on your windows while you wash them.

Stack dirty dishes in sink along with detergent and hot water if unable to wash right away.

Sewing Tips

Keep a magnet in your sewing kit. When someone spills pins or needles, simply sweep the magnet across the floor to pick up the spills.

Braided rugs often rip apart. Instead of trying to sew them, use a clear fabric glue to repair them.

Use a dry soap scrap to trace around patterns onto fabrics. Table knives are great to hold the pattern down on the fabric. They save a lot of time and pins.

To remove creases from hems, sponge material with a white vinegar solution and press flat.

To test iron temperature before ironing knits, set iron on folded paper towel. If the towel scorches or turns brown, it is too hot.

Miscellaneous Tips and Hints

To ward off tomato hornworms, sprinkle cornmeal around the plant.

Hydrogen peroxide will take out mild scorch spots. Daub it on the spot using a cotton ball, cover the spot with a cloth, and iron over it.

A handy tool in the house is a crochet hook. Keep it handy for unplugging sink traps, etc.

To comb out tangled hair, use baby lotion.

Cut flowers will last longer in a vase if ¼ tsp. or 20 drops of Clorox bleach is added to each quart of water.

Have a bar of soap handy when changing baby's diaper. If the pins don't go through easily, stick them into the soap, and they will slide very easily.

Approximate 100 Calorie Portions

Almonds (shelled) — 12 to 15 nuts
Angel cake — 1¾-inch cube
Apple — 1 large
Apple pie — ⅓ normal piece
Apricots — 5 large
Asparagus — 20 large stalks
Bananas — 1 medium
Beans — ⅓ cup canned baked
Beans, green string — 2½ cup
Beets — 1⅓ c. sliced
Bread, all kinds — slice ½-inch thick
Butter — 1 tablespoon
Buttermilk — 1⅛ cups
Cabbage — 4 to 5 cups shredded
Cake — 1¾-inch cube
Candy — 1-inch cube
Cantaloupe — 1 medium
Carrots — 1⅔ cups
Cauliflower — 1 small head
Celery — 4 cups
Cereal, uncooked— ¾ cup
Cheese — 1⅛-inch cube
Cherries, sweet fresh — 20 cherries
Cookies — 1 3-inches in diameter
Corn — ⅓ cup
Cottage cheese — 5 tablespoons
Crackers — 4 soda crackers
Crackers, graham — 2½ crackers
Cream, thick — 1 tablespoon
Cream, thin — 4 tablespoons
Cream sauce — 4 tablespoons
Dates — 3 to 4
Doughnuts — ½ doughnut
Eggs — 1⅓ eggs
Fish — fat — size of 1 chop
Fish — lean — size of 2 chops
Flour — 4 tablespoons
French dressing — 1½ tablespoons
Grape juice — ½ cup
Grapefruit juice — ½ cup
Grapes — 20 grapes
Gravy — 2 tablespoons
Ice cream — ¼ cup
Lemons — 3 large
Lettuce — 2 large heads

Macaroni — ¾ cup cooked
Malted milk — 3 tablespoons
Marmalade and jelly — 1 tablespoon
Marshmallows — 5 marshmallows
Mayonnaise — 1 tablespoon
Meat, cold sliced — ⅛-inch slice
Meat — fat — size of ½ chop
Meat — lean — size of 1 chop
Milk — ⅝ cup
Molasses — 1½ tablespoons
Onions — 3 to 4 medium
Oranges — 1 large
Orange juice — 1 cup
Peaches — 3 medium fresh
Peanut butter — 1 tablespoon
Pears — 2 medium fresh
Peas — ¾ cup canned
Pecans — 12 meats
Pie — ¼ ordinary serving
Pineapple — 2 slices, 1-inch thick
Plums — 3 to 4 large
Popcorn — 1½ cups
Potatoes, sweet — ½ medium
Potatoes, white — 1 medium
Potato salad — 1 cup
Prunes, dried — 4 medium
Radishes — 3 dozen red button
Raisins — ¼ cup seeded
Rhubarb, stewed and sweetened — ½ cup
Rice, cooked — ¾ cup
Rolls — 1 medium
Rutabagas — 1⅔ cups
Sauerkraut — 2½ cups
Sherbet — 4 tablespoons
Spinach — 2½ cups
Squash — 1 cup
Strawberries — 1⅓ cups
Sugar, brown — 3 tablespoons
Sugar, white — 2 tablespoons
Tomatoes, canned — 2 cups
Tomatoes, fresh — 2 to 3 medium
Turnips — 2 cups
Walnuts — 8 to 16 meats
Watermelon — ¾ slice, 6 inches in diameter

The Authentic Amish Cookbook

Approximate Amounts to Serve 50 People

Navy beans for baking	3 qt. or 6 lb.
Canned string beans	2 No. 10 cans
Canned beets	2 No. 10 cans
Roast beef	20 lb.
Roast beef for Swiss steak ¾ inch thick	20 lb.
Ground meat	10 lb.
Butter	1½ lb.
Chicken (roasted)	30 lb.
Chicken pie	20 lb.
Coffee	1 lb.
Baked Ham	2 hams, 10 to 12 lb. each
Ice cream — dessert	2 gal.
Ice cream — for pie	1 gal.
Lettuce	1 oz. per person
Head lettuce salad	7 lb.
Salted nuts	1½ lb.
Olives	2 qt.
Oysters (escalloped)	1 gal.
Peas	2 No. 10 cans
Peas and carrots	1 No. 10 can and 5 lb. carrots
Roast pork or fresh ham	20 lb.
Pork chops	18 lb.
Potatoes (mashed)	1¼ pecks (2½ gallons)
Sweet potatoes	13½ lb.
Rice	3 lb.
Rolls	100 rolls
Soup	3 gal.
Turkey	22 to 25 lb.
Vegetables (fresh): beans, beets, carrots, or cabbage	10 lb.
Whipped cream	2 pt.

Abbreviations Commonly Used

tsp. - teaspoon
T. - tablespoon
c. - cup
pt. - pint
qt. - quart
pk. - peck
bu. - bushel

oz. - ounce or ounces
lb. - pound or pounds
sq. - square
min. - minute or minutes
hr. - hour or hours
mod. - moderate or moderately
doz. - dozen

Simplified Measures

dash = less than ⅛ teaspoon
3 teaspoons = 1 tablespoon
16 tablespoons = 1 cup
1 cup = ½ pint
2 cups = 1 pint

2 pints (4 cups) = 1 quart
4 quarts (liquid) = 1 gallon
8 quarts (solid) = 1 peck
4 pecks = 1 bushel
16 ounces = 1 pound

If you want to measure partial cups by the tablespoon, remember:

4 tablespoons = ¼ cup
5⅓ tablespoons = ⅓ cup
8 tablespoons = ½ cup

10⅔ tablespoons = ⅔ cup
12 tablespoons = ¾ cup
14 tablespoons = ⅞ cup

Equivalent Measures and Weights

3 teaspoons = 1 tablespoon
4 tablespoons = ¼ cup
16 tablespoons = 1 cup
½ cup = 1 gill
4 gills = 1 pint
2 cups = 1 pint

4 cups = 1 quart
2 pints = 1 quart
4 quarts = 1 gallon
8 quarts = 1 peck
4 pecks = 1 bushel
16 ounces = 1 pound

Substitutions and Equivalents

2 tablespoons of fat = 1 ounce
1 cup of fat = ½ pound
1 pound of butter = 2 cups
1 cup of hydrogenated fat plus ½ tsp. salt = 1 cup butter
2 cups sugar = 1 pound
2½ cups packed brown sugar = 1 pound
1⅓ cups packed brown sugar = 1 cup of granulated sugar
3½ cups of powdered sugar = 1 pound
4 cups sifted all-purpose flour = 1 pound
4½ cups sifted cake flour = 1 pound
1 ounce bitter chocolate = 1 square
4 tablespoons cocoa plus 2 teaspoons butter = 1 ounce bitter chocolate
1 cup egg whites = 8 to 10 whites
1 cup egg yolks = 12 to 14 yolks
1 tablespoon cornstarch = 2 tablespoons flour for thickening
1 tablespoon vinegar or lemon juice + 1 cup milk =
    1 cup sour milk
1 cup whipping cream = 2 cups whipped
1 cup evaporated milk = 3 cups whipped
1 lemon = 3 to 4 tablespoons juice
1 orange = 6 to 8 tablespoons juice
1 cup uncooked rice = 3 to 4 cups cooked rice

General Oven Chart

General Oven Chart

   Very Slow Oven — 250° to 300°
   Slow Oven — 300° to 325°
   Moderate Oven — 325° to 375°
   Medium Hot Oven — 375° to 400°
   Hot Oven — 400° to 450°
   Very Hot Oven — 450° to 500°

Breads

Baking Powder Biscuits	450° 12-15 minutes
Muffins	400° to 425° 20-25 minutes
Quick Breads	350° 40-60 minutes
Yeast Bread	375° to 400° 45-60 minutes
Yeast Rolls	400° 15-20 minutes

Cakes

Butter Loaf Cakes	350° 45-60 minutes
Butter Layer Cakes	350° to 375° 25-35 minutes
Cupcakes	375° 20-25 minutes
Chiffon Cakes	325° 60 minutes
Sponge Cakes	325° 60 minutes
Angel Food Cakes	325° 60 minutes

Cookies

Bar Cookies	350° 25-30 minutes
Drop Cookies	350° to 375° 8-12 minutes
Rolled and Ref. Cookies	350° to 400° 8-12 minutes

Pastry

Meringues	350° 12-20 minutes
Pie Shells	450° 12-15 minutes
Filled Pies	450° 10 minutes, lower to 350° 40 minutes

Roasts

Beef Roast	325°	Rare 18-20 minutes per lb.
		Medium 22-25 minutes per lb.
		Well Done 30 minutes per lb.
Chicken	325° to 350° 30 minutes per lb.	
Duck	325° to 350° 25 minutes per lb.	
Fish Fillets	500° 15-20 minutes	
Goose	325° to 350° 30 minutes per lb.	
Lamb	300° to 350° 35 minutes per lb.	
Meat Loaf	375° 60 minutes for 2-lb. loaf	
Turkey	250° to 325° 15-25 minutes per lb.	
Veal Roast	300° 30 minutes per lb.	
Venison	350° 20-25 minutes per lb.	

$\mathcal{I}$ndex

Pies

Cakes, Cookies, and Frostings

Candies and Snacks

Canning and Freezing

Main Dishes

Desserts

Miscellaneous Recipes